D1389885

THE HIDDEN LIVES OF

JACK
THE
RIPPER'S
VICTIMS

For Anna

THE HIDDEN LIVES OF
JACK
THE
RIPPER'S
VICTIMS

ROBERT HUME

PEN & SWORD
HISTORY

AN IMPRINT OF PEN & SWORD BOOKS LTD.
YORKSHIRE – PHILADELPHIA

First published in Great Britain in 2019 by
PEN AND SWORD HISTORY
An imprint of
Pen & Sword Books Ltd
Yorkshire - Philadelphia

Copyright © Robert Hume, 2019

ISBN 978 1 52673 860 8

Typeset in Times New Roman 11.5/14 by
Aura Technology and Software Services, India
Printed and bound in the UK by TJ International Ltd.

Pen & Sword Books Ltd incorporates the Imprints of Pen & Sword Books
Archaeology, Atlas, Aviation, Battleground, Discovery, Family History, History,
Maritime, Military, Naval, Politics, Railways, Select, Transport, True Crime,
Fiction, Frontline Books, Leo Cooper, Praetorian Press, Seaforth Publishing,
Wharncliffe and White Owl.

For a complete list of Pen & Sword titles please contact
PEN & SWORD BOOKS LIMITED
47 Church Street, Barnsley, South Yorkshire, S70 2AS, England
E-mail: enquiries@pen-and-sword.co.uk
Website: www.pen-and-sword.co.uk

Or
PEN AND SWORD BOOKS
1950 Lawrence Rd, Havertown, PA 19083, USA
E-mail: Uspen-and-sword@casematepublishers.com
Website: www.penandswordbooks.com

Contents

Acknowledgements

I would like to thank my former pupils, who were fascinated and appalled by the Jack the Ripper murders and the mystery surrounding the suspects. It was they who inspired me to write this book about the victims themselves, and have spurred me on by asking me in the street from time to time whether I had finished it yet.

Many librarians and archivists helped with my research. In particular, I wish to thank the staff of several London libraries: the National Archives, Kew; the London Metropolitan Archives; the British Library; the Minet Library, Camberwell; and those at the public libraries in Lavender Hill and Clapham Junction. Christine Wagg, archivist at the Peabody housing association helped me with tenant registers, photographs and floor plans. Outside London, the staff of Limerick Local Studies Library; Cathays Branch and Heritage Library, Cardiff; the Templeman Library, University of Kent; and Wolverhampton Local Studies Library have also greatly helped.

I also owe thanks to Sophia Tobin, author of *Sunday Times* bestsellers *The Silversmith's Wife* and *The Widow's Confession,* for offering to comment on an early draft; and to Anna who helped me check through the proofs and compile the index.

Finally I would like to acknowledge the support team at Pen and Sword who helped get the book published: not least Claire Hopkins, who commissioned the proposal, production manager Janet Brookes and copy-editor Graham Smith.

List of Illustrations

No. 13 Miller's Court, off Dorset Street, where Mary Jane Kelly lived, and was murdered.

Glamorganshire and Monmouthshire Infirmary and Dispensary.

Artist Walter Sickert (1860–1942), named as Jack the Ripper by author Patricia Cornwell.

A 'gay house', or brothel, at 28 Collingham Place, near Earl's Court underground station.

Ratcliff Highway, St George-in-the-East, 1896.

The archway connecting Dorset Street with Miller's Court.

No. 13 Miller's Court (close-up shot).

Police photograph of Mary Jane Kelly's body on the bed at 13 Miller's Court.

Introduction

In the autumn of 1888 the 'Whitechapel Murderer' brought terror to London's East End by attacking women and severing their throats. All the murders took place within three hundred yards of one another, in some of the capital's most wretched backstreets, crowded with tenements often comprising a single room. Most of these were occupied by 'casuals' – dock labourers, market porters, hawkers and costermongers, men with no fixed wages, who might make a good deal one day, and next to nothing the day after. Not only did they expect their wives to scrub, bake and mend, but to supplement the family income by charring – doing other people's cleaning and domestic work. Writing under the pseudonym John Law in *A City Girl* (1887), Margaret Harkness describes these women as 'little better than beasts of burden'.

This was the backdrop against which the lives of at least five women ended in the most horrific of circumstances. Mary Ann Nichols was found with her throat cut in Buck's Row on 31 August. The mutilated body of Annie Chapman was discovered on 8 September in a backyard in Hanbury Street. Elizabeth Stride and Catherine Eddowes were murdered on the same night, 30 September, the one outside a club in Berner Street, the other in a corner of Mitre Square; and twenty-five-year-old Mary Jane Kelly was butchered on her own bed in Miller's Court on 9 November.

The attacks sent shock waves through not merely the East End but the whole of the Victorian metropolis. Londoners at that time were used to murders, but not to serial killers. Assuming contemporary sources can be trusted, the result was hysteria. 'No servant-maid deemed her life safe if she ventured out to post a letter after ten o'clock at night', wrote Scotland Yard's Sir Melville Macnaghten[1].

Newspapers headlined the 'barbarous outrage' and referred to 'terrible murder and mutilation'. The 'New Journalism' of the times dwelt on sensational crimes, and was keen to expose social ills. Reporters were ready to ascribe almost any murder to the hand of Jack the Ripper, a maniac who was on the loose, driven by bloodlust.

Correspondents demanded that the police solve the crimes as a matter of urgency. But the force was suffering from a severe lack of manpower. In the departments which investigated the Jack the Ripper murders, the shortage of officers was especially acute. Nor did they have the kind of forensic techniques that are available today, when fingerprinting is used as a matter of course, and DNA is routinely taken from the crime scene.

In 1888 the police had little experience in handling crime, especially one carried out in the depths of the night close to a myriad of unlit, winding alleyways, where any would-be attacker might waylay their victims, and simply melt away into the darkness.

That said, the investigation was poorly co-ordinated, and the murders were not even all handled by the same force. Catherine ('Kate') Eddowes was murdered in Mitre Square, which lies across the border in the City of London, and consequently fell within the jurisdiction of the City police, whereas the other killings came within the remit of the Metropolitan Police. Considerable time was wasted by assuming that the killer was local, while other leads were ignored. Officers came in for heavy criticism: *The East London Advertiser* condemned the Detective Department at Scotland Yard for being 'in an utterly hopeless and worthless condition'. The press abroad was even more scathing. *The New York Times* informed its readers: 'The London police and detective force is probably the stupidest in the world....'

Concerned that too little was being done to find the killer, and that the murders were damaging business in the area, a group of volunteers was formed. Led by local builder George Lusk, and calling itself the Whitechapel Vigilance Committee, members took the law into their own hands and began patrolling the streets at night.

The committee and the police placed various suspects in the frame: schoolteacher Montague John Druitt; Polish immigrants Seweryn Klosowski and Aaron Kosminski; Russian con man and thief Michael Ostrog; Francis Tumblety, a medical doctor; and John Pizer ('Leather Apron'), a local man with a history of violence against prostitutes.

Public opinion added the names of the abortionist Dr Thomas Neill Cream; medical student Thomas Hayne Cutbush; and Frederick Bailey Deeming, who later confessed to being Jack the Ripper.

An early theory shared by police and the public was that one of the local street gangs operating in the area at that time – such as The Blind Beggar Mob, The Hoxton High Rips, or The Green Gate Gang – had perpetrated the murders when their victims did not respond to blackmail threats.

Despite all this speculation, the Whitechapel Murderer was never caught. The killer's identity remains a mystery to this day, and continues to inspire a relentless flow of books, films and television programmes. Every evening, whatever the weather, packs of tourists converge on the area close to Aldgate East tube station to set off on Jack the Ripper Walks, led by guides who can supply no end of gory detail.

The vast majority of studies being published focus on possible suspects: indeed, scarcely a year goes by without a new theory emerging about who the murderer might have been. A couple of dozen individuals have been suggested, including a Liverpool cotton merchant, James Maybrick; Whitechapel mortuary attendant, Robert Mann; painter Walter Sickert; author Lewis Carroll; the fifth victim's estranged husband, Francis Spurzheim Craig; even a member of the British royal family, the Duke of Clarence; and Queen Victoria's elderly surgeon, Sir William Gull.

These conjectures have been accompanied by a stream of sensational films about Jack the Ripper, containing lurid descriptions of the murders and mutilations, and full of historical inaccuracies. The victims, whose real names have usually been changed, are frequently cast as figures of fun, misfits or freaks, as in *Jack the Ripper* (1959), where they are depicted staggering around drunk and are the only characters speaking in Cockney. In the 1988 *Jack the Ripper* TV series (featuring Michael Caine), Catherine Eddowes is shown wearing a fashionable bustle dress completely at odds with the lifestyle of a woman reduced to living in common lodging-houses and tramping through Kent to earn a few pennies from hop-picking. In *From Hell,* starring Johnny Depp (2002), the women – dressed in slashed bright red, blue and orange dresses – chat together on street corners, and sit around a table in *The Ten Bells* in Commercial Street, having a laugh, as if they were a close-knit group of friends. Yet, as far as we are aware, only Annie Chapman and Mary Jane Kelly might have met. The film gives the impression that Kelly grew up on a farm in Ireland, which she did not, and that the other women were local, which they were not. There is little or no sense of hardship, and we are told nothing about how they arrived on the streets of Whitechapel. Bizarrely, the film also casts Swedish-born Elizabeth Stride as a lesbian.

Very few serious studies have been made of the victims themselves. Many middle-class contemporaries dismissed them as the very dregs of humanity: 'filthy whores' and 'vermin', 'wantons', women who led 'very questionable' lives, threatened the institution of the family, and spread venereal disease through their 'intemperate habits' and 'irregular life'. A leading criminal anthropologist claimed that: 'Professional prostitutes are incomplete beings... they bear signs of physical and psychological degeneration that demonstrate their imperfect evolution.'[2]

By ignoring these women's pasts and the hardships they faced, some writers have unwittingly accepted the Victorian stereotype of the evil fallen woman who ultimately got what she deserved.

A recent pop-up museum (*East End Women: The Real Story*), housed in the church of St George-in-the-East, formed part of a long-term project to listen to the voices of East End women. Instead of featuring screaming victims under a blood-smeared logo, as does another local museum, it intended to draw attention to the vulnerable women who fell prey to a serial killer.

In keeping with this spirit, the present study attempts to pave the way towards a more empathetic understanding of the victims long before they reached Whitechapel. The volume aims to reveal the hidden – and much less widely known – past of these women, and considers what drove them into prostitution. It is rooted in the context of the 1880s, a period of deep economic recession, when jobs were hard to come by, and dockers were demanding their 'tanner'. Such work as was available for women was especially poorly paid. In 1888, the year of the Ripper killings, some 1,400 women and teenage girls working a fourteen-hour shift at Bryant & May's factory in Bow went on strike for higher wages, shorter hours and safer working conditions.

This book offers a contribution to help understand better the wretched lives of East End women. It questions the Victorian image of a prostitute as a bad woman who had chosen a drunken, dishonest and immoral lifestyle in preference to a sober, regular and respectable one. Jack the Ripper's victims were, in reality, ordinary working-class women with husbands, or in shared practical relationships where they pooled everything they owned. They were good-natured, had families and friends, and shared everyday ambitions and frustrations.

To the Whitechapel poor, the women were not depraved outcasts but well-known and well-liked members of their community. Mary Ann Nichols is described as 'a very clean woman', 'too good' to have any enemies but 'weighed down' by trouble; Annie Chapman as 'very respectable', an 'industrious' woman who 'never used bad language'; Elizabeth Stride as 'very poor', 'very quiet', and 'sober'; Catherine Eddowes as hardworking, 'very jolly', and 'always singing'; and Mary Jane Kelly as vivacious, 'well-educated', 'genteel', generous and 'compassionate', a woman who 'took pride in her appearance'.

Although scarcely angels, these women were trying hard to survive poverty independently, by taking on any casual work that became available. Homeless and without support, their gradual move into prostitution was not due to laziness or depravity, but personal circumstances: betrayal, bereavement, unemployment, domestic violence, or a simple mistake here

Map showing the locations of the murders.

and there. Given the limited options available to them – beyond extremely badly paid needlework or piecework in sweatshops – prostitution was a rational choice among a series of unpleasant alternatives for women: a means of survival.

This is not 'yet another book' about Jack the Ripper. Its purpose is to move the spotlight away from the murderer to where it has so far barely been placed, on the obscure lives of the victims.

Chapter 1

Mary Ann Nichols
('Polly')

Charles Andrew Cross woke in the small hours each morning to go to work at Pickfords, where he had been a removal man for over twenty years.

About half-past three on Friday 31 August 1888, as he was passing through Buck's Row, Whitechapel, an object caught his eye on the opposite side of the road, lying against the gateway. At first it seemed like a tarpaulin sheet. But as he drew closer he realised that it was a body.

An instant later he heard the footsteps of a man approaching.

'Come and look over here', Cross called out: 'there is a woman lying on the pavement.'

The two men went over to the body. Cross took hold of the woman's hands. They were cold and limp: 'I believe she is dead', he said.

The man who had joined him placed his hand on her heart. 'No, I think she is breathing.'

Cross suggested they prop her up, but the other man refused to touch her.

The night being very dark, neither of them noticed that the woman's throat had been cut.

They ran to fetch a policeman, to report that they had seen a woman lying in Buck's Row – 'either drunk or dead'.[1]

The dead woman was identified as forty-three-year-old Mary Ann Nichols, known to everyone by her pet name, 'Polly' – the wished-for child. She had been born on 26 August 1845, to locksmith Edward Walker and his wife, Caroline.

As a young girl, she had lived just outside the city wall at Dawes Court, which lay in a turning off Shoe Lane, close to the River Fleet, on the main route linking Holborn's famous inns of court to Fleet Street with its busy newspaper industry.

By 1851 Polly was living a three-minute walk away at 14 Dean Street, off Fetter Lane, with her brothers: Edward, two years older than her,

Buck's Row (now Durward Street), Whitechapel, where Mary Ann Nichols was murdered (Wikimedia Commons).

Discovering Mary Ann Nichols's body in Buck's Row (reproduced in *Docklands & East London Advertiser* online 31 Aug. 2013).[2]

and Frederick, four years her junior. Mrs Walker worked from home as a laundress[3], a backbreaking job that involved carrying into the house heavy bundles of dirty sheets and clothes to wash by hand. She would wring them out using a mangle, dry the clothes in the yard, iron them, and return them to customers neatly pressed. Maybe it was when she was helping her mother that Polly fell and cut her forehead, which left her with a scar for the rest of her life.

Mary Ann Nichols ('Polly')

Polly, Edward and their father, a powerfully built man with a greying beard, were living nearby at 19 Harp Alley in 1861.[4] Her mother was dead, so was Polly's little brother, Frederick, who had died when he was two years old. That was the way of the world at this time, when the average life expectancy in England was only about forty years. Unlike today, women tended to die younger than men, frequently succumbing to infection during childbirth; and babies, brought up in cold and damp conditions, were highly susceptible to the killer diseases of the day, such as scarlet fever, measles, and whooping cough. Younger children were especially vulnerable; and even when the sickness was not fatal, it always left them in a weakened state.[5]

Over the next few years, her father managed to better himself by setting up as a blacksmith with his own shop and furnace, forging a wide range of products, from simple horseshoes to fancy iron gates.

Fifteen-year-old Polly was expected to take on all the duties of her dead mother. This meant shopping and cooking, and all the housework, which entailed scrubbing floors, lighting fires and clearing ashes from grates. She would be required to grow up fast.

It was perhaps one morning, as she sat on the front step to take a breather, that she caught sight of a rather handsome young man on his way to work. William Nichols, who was three years older than Polly, lived close by in Bouverie Street. He had once worked as a warehouseman in Oxford, but was now a printer's machinist at Messrs Perkins, Bacon & Co. in Fleet Street, a printer of books, banknotes and postage stamps – notably the Penny Black.

Polly no doubt saw William Nichols as a good catch with pleasing prospects. Here was a man who could rescue her from the daily drudgery in her father's house, where to all intents and purposes she was no more than a domestic servant.

Nichols was in all likelihood attracted by this bubbly young woman with her high cheekbones, glossy brown hair and big brown eyes, who would generally call out some saucy remark or other as he passed by.

Quite possibly she asked him to walk with her. There were various garden squares and the Inner Temple Gardens a short distance away, where they might have sat and talked. Or maybe she invited him for a drink at the local hostelry, the *Hops and Grapes*.

Perhaps the pair of them could set up home one day, somewhere small, but at least a place they might call their own, where they would be free to do as they pleased.

Although the couple were regularly seen together, it must have come as a surprise to friends and relatives when they suddenly announced their intention to tie the knot.

On 16 January 1864, William and Polly, still only nineteen-years-old, were married in St Bride's, the so-called 'printers' church', in Fleet Street.[6]

The newly-weds lived briefly with his family at 30 Bouverie Street, close to the Fleet Street offices of the *Daily News,* which Charles Dickens edited. The house was large, having been built on the site of Whitefriars Priory, and possessed an ancient crypt beneath, but the upper floors were too small for all of them.

After a few months they crossed the Thames and moved in with her father who now had a place at 131 Trafalgar Street, Walworth Road, a grand thoroughfare boasting some 'elegant villas'. It was scarcely the house of her own that she probably hoped for, but at least they now had more space.

They remained there for the next twelve years and raised a family.

With little birth control available, Victorian couples tended to have many more children than those today – on average at least six. Besides, they knew that half were unlikely to reach their fifth birthday.[7] A son, Edward John Nichols, was born in 1866, and two years later a second son, Percy George, arrived, followed by a daughter, Alice Esther, in 1870.

Meanwhile, the adults in the family were prospering. Her brother, Edward, was doing well as an engineer, and could afford to marry. On Christmas Day 1869, William and Polly had attended his wedding to Mary Anne Ward at St Peter's Church in Walworth.

William Nichols also had steady work as a printer, and he and Polly could, at last, think about finding a place of their own to live.

On 31 July 1876, they were accepted as tenants in Peabody Buildings, Duke (now Duchy) Street, Lambeth, close to the Thames, and Waterloo railway station. The new five-storey complex, financed by American entrepreneur and philanthropist George Peabody (1795–1869)[8], lay just behind Stamford Street in what had been a 'back-slum'. Designed by Henry Astley Darbishire of Trafalgar Square, it was one of an eventual thirty or so to be constructed in London, and consisted of a large yellow-brick housing estate with white arches, surrounded by iron railings. Peabody intended that respectable working-class folk of good moral character occupy the dwellings, though in practice well-to-do artisans and mechanics were sometimes admitted, along with their pianos.

Peabody had made his money in the grocery trade, but he never forgot his humble origins as one of eight children born to a poor family, and before retiring he had discussed with friends a suitable gift for the poor working families of London. One possibility was a donation towards building more ragged schools for destitute children; another, to replace houses that had been demolished when the railways were constructed; a third, to build a network of clean drinking water fountains to help alleviate cholera.

When he decided to do none of these, but instead donate £150,000 to provide affordable housing for the London poor, it caused great excitement in the capital.

Peabody's trustees decided to admit to the dwellings workmen and their families who were in employment but had very low incomes (the so-called 'deserving poor'), in other words, those who were already doing something to help themselves, but could do with some extra support. 'They will never save their children from the dreadful and unnatural mortality now prevalent', argued Peabody, 'or save themselves from untimely sickness and death, until they have cheap pure water in unlimited quantity, wholesome air, efficient drainage.'[9]

Only clean living conditions would combat filth, disease, immorality and what many contemporaries believed to be the apathetic stupor of slum dwellers. Therefore, in all Peabody buildings, blocks were separated from one another to allow good ventilation, and every resident was vaccinated against smallpox.

William and Polly were exactly the kind of people Peabody proposed should benefit from his legacy – Londoners either 'by birth or residence', and a 'good member of society'. Their new home was Tenement No. 3, on the ground floor of Block D, one of twenty blocks. It was one of the largest apartments in the complex, and comprised four rooms. The rent was 6 shillings and 8 pence per week, and rates 1 shilling and 7 pence, a sum that Nichols was able to afford because he now earned 30 shillings per week since his promotion to printer at William Clowes and Sons, type music and general printers of Duke Street. The company had been thriving since receiving a commission to print half a million catalogues for London's Great Exhibition of 1851, and his job seemed secure.[10]

Newspapers were highly complimentary about the various Peabody estates, one describing the apartments as 'wonderful mansions'.[11] Floors were properly boarded, walls cemented, and 'all are at present beautifully white'. A fireplace had been installed in each room, and in the kitchen an oven and boiler, large cupboards and ample shelving. On each landing, the builder, William Cubitt & Co. of Grays Inn Road, had constructed a dust chute for waste: 'the tenants having no further trouble than to open it and drop down the contents of their shovel'. A bin 'of neat and ingenious construction', supposed to be capable of holding half a ton of coal, was also located in the passage outside.

'The early estates did not provide self-contained flats; they were what was known as "associated dwellings"', writes Peabody Archivist, Christine Wagg.[12] The couple would have shared access with other families to a laundry and drying room at the top of the block, where could be found a wringing-machine, four tubs with water taps above each, and three large coppers – each family being allocated one day a week for washing. Another room on the ground floor housed a bath, which William and Polly would have been able to use without charge as often as they pleased – they just had to pick up the key at the superintendent's office. Gas heating on the estates was provided in the washhouses, and gas lighting on the staircases and entrance ways, all at the trustees' expense.

The couple had no sink or lavatory of their own, needing to share those on the landing with another family, and take turns cleaning them. It was also their responsibility to keep the laundry windows 'free from dirt',

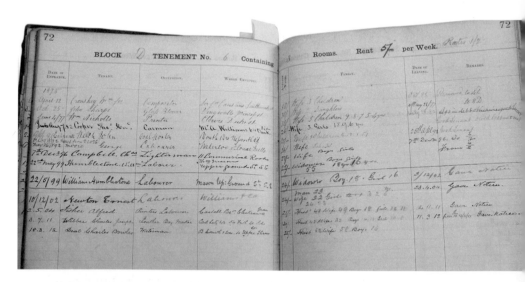

William Nichols's entry (third line down) in the tenant register of the Peabody ('Stamford') Estate, Duke Street, 4 June 1877. It marked the family's move from Tenement 3 on the ground floor of Block D, to Tenement 6 on the first floor. The five-storey block was demolished in the 1970s. (© Peabody, London)

sweep the passages and steps every morning, and beat their carpets. They were warned that regular inspections would be made to check they were keeping their facilities up to scratch.

Everyone seemed to be living on top of everyone else, and sharing so many things with strangers took some getting accustomed to. The only person Polly had been used to sharing anything with had been her father, whose ways she had often disliked but had come to accept.[13]

Although the estate was criticised by some for its austere, even brutal appearance – a 'strange mix of workhouse and barracks', with long corridors, railings that separated the building from surrounding streets, and gates that were locked at 11 p.m. – William and Polly at least now had their independence, away from their parents.

How fortune had favoured them. Who knew what further blessings lay just around the corner?

For a while they appear to have been happy.

Their fellow residents were an ecclectic mix of labourers and porters, coachmen and bookbinders, messengers and hatters, tailors, and printers like Nichols. They could be heard racing down the stairs to work in the morning, and returning, often the worse for drink, late at night. From the other tenements came raised voices, the sound of scraping furniture, the crashes of objects being dropped.

Next door to them, at No. 5, lived a widow who had moved to London from Hampshire. Mrs Sarah Vidler had three children, one of which, Rosetta Walls, had separated from her husband. Rosetta was now eking out a living by cleaning people's houses, and nursing – even though she had received no medical training.

This striking young woman in her early twenties – almost ten years younger than Polly – quickly turned William's head.

When Polly was laid up with her fourth child, Rosetta came in to help nurse her.

Before long his interest developed into infatuation. William Nichols was smitten. For him, the young woman would have been everything that his wife was when they first met: lively, full of energy, exciting.

By the time baby Eliza Sarah was born in December 1876, the Nichols had started to quarrel, and Polly had begun drinking gin. Its bitter taste and powerful effects were so addictive that it had acquired the notorious nickname 'Mother's Ruin' – because women were prone to neglect their children for the sake of a tipple.

Polly may well have called it by one of its other appellations: 'a flash of lightning'. The strong liquor energised her, and gave instant release from what had become a miserable life of continous childbearing to a man who seemed to have lost interest in her.

One day, befuddled by drink, she tottered into the road in Lambeth, straight into the path of a passing cab.[14] The vehicle veered just in time; but a glancing blow from one of its lamps led to a second nasty gash on her forehead. She was taken to St Thomas's Hospital, the wound was stitched, and she returned home that evening. William was angry when he learnt the cause of the accident, and there was an unpleasant scene. He told his friends that the drink was sending her 'raving mad'. If it had not been for her drinking habits, he said, 'they would have got on all right together'.[15]

When the soporific effects of the gin began to lessen, Polly's mood changed and she generally became irritable and prone to pick arguments. She would accuse her husband of spending too much time with Rosetta, instead of being there for her and the children.

During one of these outbursts she walked out, and went to live with the only other person who could provide a roof over her head – her father.

By early February 1877 she had returned to William, and the family was together again. But it was proving difficult to feed four children on William's wages, and they decided to move into cheaper accommodation at No. 6, the other side of Mrs Vidler and Rosetta. Seeing as they now occupied three rooms rather than four, the rent was only 5 shillings per week, and the rates only 1 shilling and 2 pence.

For the next year or so, William and Polly managed to get along – on and off – but the following summer, as Prime Minister Benjamin Disraeli was threatening war with Russia, tempers also flared again in Duke Street.

In truth, the couple had not been getting along too well for some years, long before Rosetta Walls had caught the printer's eye.

But for Polly it was simple: William had betrayed her.

Polly took flight again, leaving the children in her husband's custody – all but their eldest son, Edward John, who went to live with his grandfather.

Without an allowance coming in from William, Polly needed to earn a few pennies of her own.

But this proved much more difficult than she had reckoned. In the recession that was gripping not just Britain but Europe and the US, there were simply too many women chasing too few jobs. Such as did become available were quickly grabbed by the men – often those arriving from Ireland, which was caught up in another famine; or Jews fleeing from persecution in Russia's pogroms. Unable to find more than the odd day's cleaning, she became increasingly desperate.

By this time Polly was heavily pregnant again. The thought of returning to her husband would doubtless have made her cringe. Her only chance was the workhouse.

Having satisfied the guardians that she was a deserving case, she was admitted to Lambeth Workhouse, Renfrew Road. A 'Mary Ann Nichols, charwoman', aged thirty-five, is recorded on the admission list of 'inmates' (as the paupers were known) on 17 August 1878.[16]

In many respects her new temporary home bore striking similarities with the Peabody Estate. It was built from the same dirty yellow-grey brick, had the same sash windows that rattled in the wind, keeping inmates awake at night, and dark, musty-smelling, arched entranceways. In one particular, Lambeth Workhouse actually seemed less grim because it had fewer floors, enabling more light to enter than from the Peabody courtyards.

It was standard practice in workhouses at that time to separate men and women – some said for fear of breeding more paupers. Housed in the south wing, Polly was kept apart from the men in the north, and only caught sight of one or two of them when they were

Lambeth Workhouse, Renfrew Road. (Courtesy Peter Higginbotham/workhouses. org.uk)

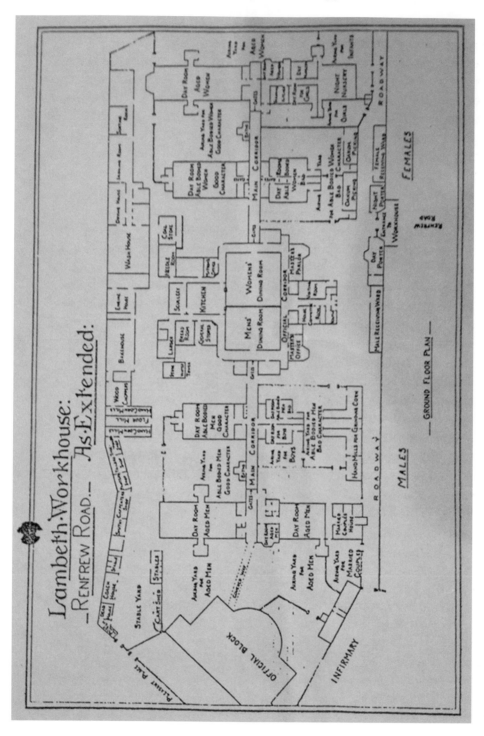

Plan of Lambeth Workhouse. (Uploaded to Flikr by Maggie Jones)

sent to do odd jobs in the women's quarters. Her meals were also eaten in an all-female dining room, where she was made to sit in a long row, shoulder to shoulder with other paupers, eating carefully measured-out food in complete silence. Having always enjoyed the company of men as much as women, she would not have liked this arrangement one bit.

As it was summer, workhouse rules required her to get up at 5 a.m. and work from 7 a.m. until midday, when she would be given dinner; and again from 1 p.m. until 6 p.m. when she would get supper. While men were employed to break stones or turn cranks to grind corn, Polly was required to clean or 'pick oakum', which involved unravelling fibres in old ships' ropes to provide material for watertight sealing. The bell for bed was rung at 8 p.m. Only Saturday evening was different, when Polly and the other inmates had to assemble to sing and recite verses. That evening also gave her an opportunity to catch up with bits of gossip, and she certainly heard plenty of stories – about a nurse who administered morphine to a patient so they would sleep, then killed them; and a previous master called Catch, or was it Patch, who was dismissed for using hydrochloric acid to smoke out a woman inmate he believed was hiding up a chimney in one of the infirm wards[17]. The women listened, with a mixture of horror and fascination. But really it was little wonder that such things went on when those who were employed in workhouses were often unsuited to their work and went about it unsupervised.

As her time drew close, Polly feared that her baby would be taken away if she gave birth in the workhouse. So, early in December she decided to return home to her husband. Perhaps things would now be different.

In 1879 she gave birth to her last son, Henry Alfred.

Nothing is known about Polly and William for the rest of the year. However, over Easter 1880 there was another huge row when Polly confronted her husband over his affair with Rosetta Walls.

When William denied he was seeing her, Polly flew into a rage, called him a liar, packed up her things and fled, leaving the children behind – even tiny Henry Alfred.

She would never return.

Although the law at that time gave husbands the right to divorce their wives on grounds of adultery, married women had no rights against their husbands going with other women.[18] Proven instances of cruelty or 'aggravated assault' were needed to accompany William's alleged infidelity; but there were none.

The best she could do in these circumstances was to separate.

But it left Polly with nothing. No income. No family to support her. No roof over her head. She was on her own.

* * *

For the next six months she somehow or other managed to scrape together a living by cleaning rich people's houses; selling watercress, violets or primroses; and when needs must, by selling herself.

On 6 September 1880 she returned to Lambeth Workhouse, her clothes were placed into store, and she was again issued with a workhouse uniform. There she remained until the last day of May 1881, in the company of more than 800 other inmates – most, like her, victims of unemployment.

William Nichols was now paying Polly maintenance – a weekly allowance of five shillings, which he was required to do by law[19]. But this payment came to an abrupt end early in 1882 when he learnt from his friends that she was making a living from prostitution.

Nichols was furious. One can imagine him seizing Polly and demanding how she could stoop so low. The woman with whom he shared his bed, the mother of his children, had offered herself to passing strangers. He was disgusted. It was something he could not accept, ever.

From now on, Polly's life would change for all time. With no income from her husband, she risked going under – sinking completely.

Friends encouraged her to issue a summons against him for maintenance, which she did. But it was a lost battle. At court, witnesses testified to her 'immoral lifestyle'[20], and she lost her case.

Polly re-admitted herself into Lambeth Workhouse on 24 April 1882. The following January, being unwell, she was sent for a couple of days to Lambeth Infirmary in Brook Drive, Kennington. This was the largest infirmary in London, with twenty-seven wards. Many of its 650 patients were suffering from consumption (TB); others were receiving mercury treatment for syphilis. It was certainly a cut above the sick wards of dirty and poorly ventilated workhouses, where the paupers themselves – some of them rough types – frequently acted as nurses.

At the Lambeth Infirmary Polly would have found the nurses diligent, kind and gentle; and the milk and beef tea she was given were much more nutritious than anything offered in workhouses. Visiting missionaries might urge inmates to mend their ways or face the tortures of hell – but no need to take notice of them, she thought. Before she knew it, she was returned to Lambeth Workhouse where she remained until the days began to lengthen.

When spring finally arrived, her father took her back, and offered to provide her with food and a room for as long as she needed.

However, her drinking caused one fall-out after another, and finally Walker 'let her go'.[21]

She could not return to her husband, even if she had wished. William Nichols had left Peabody Buildings in debt the previous summer, and was living in Bethnal Green with Rosetta Walls who was pregnant with their child – the future Arthur Nichols.

Polly needed a place to go where she could sort herself out, regain some strength, and think what to do next. Another fortnight in Lambeth Workhouse at the end of May 1883 gave her that opportunity.

Over the next four years she did her best to earn an independent livelihood. But she was canny enough to realise that should this fail she would need support from a man with a steady occupation – someone like Thomas Stuart Drew, a blacksmith who had his own shop in York Street, Walworth. His wife, Matilda, only thirty-five-years-old, had recently died, leaving him with three girls – Matilda (15), Maud (11) and Louisa (4). He sought companionship, and someone who could give him a hand with his youngest daughter.

Polly got on well with Drew. With his support, and encouraged by the sound of girls laughing as they raced around the house, Polly regained some of her former cheerfulness, perhaps also some self-confidence and pride. Fellow mourners described her as 'respectably dressed' on 5 June 1886 when she attended the funeral of her brother, Edward, who had died from burns following a terrible accident at home.[22]

Now the only Walker child still alive, Polly's life, too, was about to be cut short. Little could her father have imagined, when he saw her at Edward's funeral, that he would never speak to her again.

Like her father and her husband, Drew also soon grew tired of Polly's drinking. It was just a matter of time, she thought, before he would throw her out. On 25 October 1887 she ran off, taking with her some of his clothes, which she sold in a pawnshop and bought gin with the proceeds. From there, she seems to have gone to Trafalgar Square to 'sleep rough'.

Next day, the *Daily News* reported that a woman called Mary Ann Nichols, described by police as 'the worst woman in the square', had been arrested and taken to Bow Street police station, where she continued to behave 'very disorderly'. The woman, if it was Polly, was brought before Bow Street Magistrates' Court, where Italian adventurer and womaniser, Giacomo Casanova, had once been tried for assault. Many of the accused left the court to begin jail sentences. Charles Dickens, then a young journalist, described 'boys of ten, as hardened in vice as men of fifty… going joyfully to prison as a place for food and shelter'.[23]

However, Mary Ann Nichols was simply given a warning. The magistrate described her as 'destitute', with no means of sustenance, and ordered her return to Lambeth Workhouse to scrub floors, sew and pick oakum.

With no money for a bed in a common lodging, or 'doss' house, Polly began to drift from one workhouse to another. The matron at St Giles Workhouse in Endell Street allowed her to stay one night there, on

Bow Street Magistrates' Court, 1895. (Wikipedia)

condition that she was stripped and bathed. Her fellow inmates came from all sections of society. Although there were plenty of washerwomen, charwomen and domestic servants among their number, Polly also found herself in the company of skilled tailors, staymakers and upholsterers who had simply fallen on hard times.[24]

The following morning, Polly had to leave, though she managed to find a place in Strand Workhouse that evening. Situated in Silver Street, Edmonton, the three-storey building was to be her home for the whole of November. She tried to make new friends among paupers admitted on a daily basis; but no sooner had she got to know them when many would have been transferred to the workhouse infirmary with bronchitis, apoplexy or dropsy; and the less fortunate from there into the mortuary next door.[25]

When Polly was discharged, she again slept rough in the cold December nights in Trafalgar Square, with other homeless people. The square had long been a rallying point for demonstrations. Two Februarys before, East Enders had swarmed into the square to protest against unemployment, before marching through Pall Mall and St James's. Rich gentlemen in their clubs laughed at them. But the laughter had turned sour. Stones were thrown, windows broken, shops looted.[26] The episode confirmed the idea, already ingrained in the minds of many rich people, that all East Enders were criminals.

Only two weeks earlier, on 13 November 1887, Trafalgar Square had witnessed tens of thousands of socialists, marching to protest against unemployment. In an incident that has become known as London's 'Bloody Sunday', many were injured by police truncheons, or were trampled under the hooves of police horses.[27]

Protests continued long afterwards. The fight for women's jobs, in particular, was a cause close to Polly's heart. Assuming they were available at all, the work was menial, and very low-paid. Unable to earn an 'honest living' herself, Polly joined in the commotions enthusiastically. Yet what could change until women were given the vote?

Polly spent a further ten days in Lambeth Workhouse, including Christmas Day, when she ate a meal of roast beef and plum pudding in silence, with hundreds of other women seated in rows. It was to be her last Christmas.

* * *

William Nichols continued to do well: he had been promoted to printer at Perkins, Bacon & Co. By contrast, his wife, with no income, was seeking refuge in Mitcham Workhouse in Holborn on 4 January 1888. Concerned by her persistent cough, the matron sent her to the Holborn Union Infirmary in Highgate (Archway Hospital), a vast, turreted building with 625 beds. It must have appeared intimidating even to Polly who had sadly become a seasoned inmate of London's workhouses and infirmaries.

On her arrival, she was escorted into a two-storey block, which contained receiving wards, a doctor's residence and a dispensary. Once all the paperwork was complete, she was taken across to the women's wards in the south part. In every facet of their lives, as in the workhouses, men and women were kept apart. This included their leisure. A recreation area at the back of the Infirmary was divided up, a part for men another for women. Even sick paupers, it seemed, were thought likely to get into mischief.[28]

Anxious to prevent Polly becoming a burden on the ratepayers of Holborn, the Infirmary drew up an order of removal to her parish of settlement, and on 16 April she was sent back to Lambeth. This time she was admitted into the new tougher 'test' workhouse, built in Prince's Road to house 200 able-bodied men and 150 able-bodied women. A striking feature about her fellow inmates was that they came from hitherto steady trades that had recently gone under – among their number grocers, bricklayers, hatters and weavers.[29] In return for their food, shelter and clothes, the test workhouse required them to endure a particularly strict, and at times dangerous, programme of work. For men, it meant turning a crank to grind corn, and breaking stones, without eye protection. For women, there was oakum to pick, which left them with sore and bleeding hands.

Each sex was segregated into three classes, according to their conduct and character. Fortunately for Polly, her character and conduct was adjudged good; for those who were classified as being of bad character had to perform their work in isolation from one another.

During April and May she became friends with a Mrs Scorer – she never got to know her first name, only that she had separated from her husband, a salesman at Spitalfields Market. Also with Mary Ann Monk, described as 'a young woman with a flushed face and a haughty air'.

Impressed by Polly's good behaviour and hard work, the matron, whose name was Mrs Fielder, felt confident to recommend Polly for a situation as servant at a newly built house in Rosehill, a quiet residential street close to Wandsworth Common. A Mr Francis Cowdry owned the house, which was called 'Ingleside'.[30]

Francis and his wife, Martha, had moved into the house – which lay next door to his parents, Samuel and Sarah Cowdry [31] – from a smaller two-storey property in Belleville Road, Clapham, on the other side of the common,[32] where they had employed a fifteen-year-old girl, called Ellen, as a domestic servant. Mrs Cowdry, who was almost ten years her husband's senior, now seized the opportunity to give Ellen notice. Perhaps she found her unreliable and scatter-brained; we don't know.

Since then she had managed on her own, until she learned that good mature servants, properly trained in domestic skills, could be obtained from Lambeth Workhouse. Having been taught how to scrub, clean and do needlework, Polly was ideally suited to the situation, and she would have relished the opportunity of making a fresh start.

At least in her new place she would be spared the dreadful task of picking oakum. Nor would she have to bathe in dirty water. No more cloudy meat soup with grease on the top, no gristly meat you couldn't get your knife to cut. Mrs Cowdry surely wouldn't open her mail as they did in the workhouse. Nor check through letters before she was allowed to send them. No more singing, or saying prayers. No need to cover her ears each Sunday to block out the preacher going on and on about working hard, or going to hell.

Fate seemed to be looking kindly upon Polly, who was now forty-two years old. It seemed after all that she had turned the corner and been given another chance.

On 12 May 1888, Polly said goodbye to her friends and left Lambeth Workhouse to begin her new job for Mrs Martha Cowdry. She hastily gathered together her few possessions. As she had no underclothes of her own, the matron allowed her to take two workhouse petticoats with her.

From the moment she took up her duties, Mrs Cowdry would have made the rules of her new house abundantly clear: Polly had to get up at half past five, six o'clock on Sundays. While the mornings were still chilly she would be required to carry scuttles of coal from the basement to the ground floor dining room and drawing room, clean the chimney flues, black-lead the grate, clean the shovel, tongs and poker, and light the fires. The brass door knocker had to be polished until it gleamed, and boots and shoes cleaned. The stone floors and steps had to be scrubbed, which would mean putting up with bruised knees. In the kitchen she would have to scour the copper saucepans with silver sand, salt, vinegar and flour; and, once a week, clean the silver with borax and soap. On top of this there were errands to run, and letters to take to the post. Her days would be filled.

But she would at least have her freedom.

As Mrs Cowdry had no cook, Polly would almost certainly have been provided with a copy of Mrs Isabella Beeton's best-selling book on household management.[33] Her father had taught her to read, and the

'Ingleside', Rosehill, Wandsworth, where Polly worked as a domestic servant in 1888. The dormer window of her bedroom can be seen above. (Robert Hume)

pictures would have helped her to take in what it said. She would be expected to prepare and cook food, lay the table for dinner, wash up the dishes, and carry out the duties of a general domestic servant. It would mean being frugal. Any leftovers from the kitchen would most probably have had to stay in the house, with no taking the dripping away and selling it to other households: it was to stay on the shelf in the larder. Butter and sugar would doubtless have been locked away, and whenever they were required she would have had to ask Mrs Cowdry for the key.

When opening the door to visitors in the afternoon, she had to wear a starched apron and a cap, and see that her hair was scraped up inside. All but Sunday afternoons, that is. These were hers, as was one evening each week, and a day off once a month – though she would have had to be back by ten o'clock, not a minute later, and on no account was to bring back any 'followers'. Every Sunday evening she would have been expected to go to church.

Polly would have worked in the basement, and slept at the top of the house in a little attic room, lit by candlelight. That was sufficient illumination because an old photograph of the road shows that directly outside the house stood a gaslamp, lit every evening by a man carrying a ladder. The lamp cast a glow, albeit a dingy one, over the meagre furniture in her room: probably no more than an iron bed with a lumpy flock mattress; a mirror, tarnished with black spots; and a simple washstand, jug and chamber pot – for she would not, of course, have been allowed to use the master and mistress's lavatory.

From the window she had a fine view over Wandsworth Common with its oaks, birch trees and lakes; the Surrey Lunatic Asylum; and Wandsworth Prison (or House of Correction, as it was known) the largest prison in the country; while in the distance she could hear the whistles of steam locomotives at Clapham Junction, one of the busiest railway stations in the world.

So much activity, while 'Ingleside' stayed so quiet. It was all very different to working in a big house, where you could chat and have a laugh with the other servants. Like six out of every ten domestics in this period, Polly was the only servant in the house. At times she must have felt lonely and isolated, having left behind her friends at Lambeth Workhouse.

Except for tradesmen and visitors who came to the house, she saw little of the outside world, for Mrs Cowdry allowed her very limited free time. Still, what would she have done with it? Polly had no money to spend because servants were paid in arrears after completing three months' work. Instead she most probably wandered on the common and asked passers-by for a ha'penny. Once she had collected six of the coins she would have been able to afford to buy a 'warmer' – her 'flash of lightning'.

Maid in a pinafore: what Nichols may have looked like. (Alyson Dunlop's blog)[34]

Polly managed to keep in good spirits, and in a letter she wrote to her father in Camberwell, soon after she took up her situation, was able to joke about her drinking habits and her lack of a religious faith:

> I just write to say you will be glad to know that I am settled in my new place and going all right up to now. My people went out yesterday and have not returned so I am left in charge. It is a grand place inside with trees and gardens back and front. All has been newly done up. They are teetotallers and very religious so I ought to get on. They are very nice people and I have not much to do. I do hope you are all right and the boy [her son, Edward John] has work.
>
> So goodbye now for the present.
>
> Yours Truly Polly.
>
> Answer soon please and let me know how you are.[35]

Her father replied but received nothing in return.

On 12 July 1888, exactly two months to the day that she had begun work at 'Ingleside', Polly took flight.

A couple of days later, Lambeth Workhouse received a postcard from Martha Cowdry notifying them that her servant, Mary Ann Nichols, had absconded, stealing linen worth £3 10 shillings – more than £300 in today's values. Perhaps she had always been suspicious of employing a woman from a workhouse, even one like Polly who came with such a good reference. What had reduced her to seek refuge in such a place? Surely a woman in her mid-forties should either have been married, or found respectable employment before now? She should never have trusted her. How stupid she had been.

The truth was that Polly would have been desperate for money, for she had received nothing during the whole of her time with the Cowdrys. Servants were renown for pilfering goods such as tea and sugar from their employer's pantry or larder, and selling them to their friends and relatives to make a few pennies while they waited to be paid. Many also stole gold bracelets and rings, pearl necklaces, watches and clocks, silk dresses and linen, and pawned them to raise some cash. Polly was no exception.

Any identification mark she would have picked out of Mrs Cowdry's sheets before taking them to the pawnbroker, or 'leaving shop', and receiving a 'loan' and a ticket. It was easy enough. No questions would have been asked should a middle-aged woman be seen carrying a bundle of clothes – they were probably taking in washing. Visiting the nearest pawnshop to sell an item of clothing was a way of life, a weekly routine, for many working-class people at this time, and helped raise enough money for a day or two's food. Some urban streets are said to have had more pawnbrokers than public houses. 'Uncle', as the pawnbroker was colloquially known, could always be turned to in times of need. His customers were never those in dire poverty but those living close to the breadline that were in regular, but poorly paid work, and who owned something to offer. Clothing was often pledged on Monday and redeemed on Saturday when workers were paid, worn to church on Sunday, and pledged again the next day.

Despite the value of the sheets to Mrs Cowdry, Polly probably received a poor return for them because there were plenty of other people stealing clothes from washing lines at night and taking them to pawnbrokers. Indeed the practice was so common that the Victorian underworld even had a word for it: 'snowing'.

With whatever sum she was given, Polly made her way back towards Lambeth to wander the streets and drink away the proceeds in its public houses. At last she had a few shillings to buy a drink. In the *Crown and Anchor,* on the corner of Rodney Place and New Kent Road, she met up with her friend Mary Ann Monk who had left Lambeth Workhouse and was charring and doing odd jobs.[36]

Polly thought of doing the same. Certainly, she would not be able to return to Lambeth Workhouse: she had disgraced herself, broken the trust of the matron and become a woman of 'bad character'. She could not go back to her unfaithful husband who had moved away with his new partner; and her father would never put up with more of her drinking.

At various odd moments she would almost certainly have weighed up other possibilities. There was taking in people's washing, as her mother had done – but she had no home to take it to, no sink, no mangle, no iron. Perhaps she could go back to selling flowers or watercress, out in all weather, walking over to Covent Garden at four in the morning, like many poor children did; sort rags in a rag factory – risking infection from lice and fleas; or make matchboxes in her room by day, and much of the night, for Bryant & May of Bow – provided she was able to

21

afford her own paste. Or take up work sewing on buttons and cutting buttonholes: women, she was told, were always needed in the so-called 'slop' trade, working from home, sewing men's shirts and being paid by the piece.

Maybe she could make artificial flowers to decorate hats; or work in a sweaters' den. But the pay for items of clothing was abysmally low, the work extremely arduous, and it meant dealing with sudden orders from local factories, which carried tight deadlines. She would be working up to seventeen hours a day – even longer than what she had been doing at the Cowdrys. She had heard tales of girls throwing water into their eyes to keep themselves awake. No wonder that dressmakers looked ten years older than domestic servants when they reached their mid-thirties. Not for her. It would be like prison.[37]

By the time she got to King's Cross on the evening of 1 August she felt thoroughly exhausted and decided to queue at Gray's Inn Temporary or Casual Workhouse, where beds were generally available for one night only. The following morning she had to leave. Mary Ann Monk had suggested Polly walk to the East End where she would have a better chance of earning a few pennies cleaning houses, or selling this and that. The people were a friendly, down-to-earth lot, said Monk, with no airs and graces like the West End types, and they would soon make her feel at ease.

Although London was the wealthiest city in the world in the 1880s, it was a divided one. While the West End enjoyed the nation's wealth, the East End did not. The West was home to expensive jewellers, theatres and squares lined with elegant Georgian houses. The East End – Polly's new home – with its music halls, filthy slums and air polluted by the stench of tanneries and gasworks, was a whole world apart.

The area had gained such notoriety that during the 1880s the upper classes would go 'slumming' to see for themselves bare-footed children running about the dirty streets, which were home to a quarter of a million slum dwellers, facing an ongoing battle to make ends meet. At midnight, fashionable Londoners left their dignified homes and clubs in Mayfair and Belgravia, and crowded into omnibuses bound for the East End. One company even offered 'guided slumming tours' in order to witness the depravity and squalor first hand.[38] The upper classes could not get enough of this entertainment: they were able to sample what the poor ate by purchasing a bag of jellied eels from a street vendor, and were shown into their backyards, even into their privvies. They could also see prostitutes in the streets. Although many viewed them as objects of disgust, they were also intensely fascinated by them.

Of all the districts in the East End, Whitechapel, where Polly came to settle, was the poorest. Barrister and novelist, Bracebridge Hemyng, stated in 1861 that it was looked upon as 'a suspicious, unhealthy locality... its population a strange amalgamation of Jews, English, French, Germans, and other antagonistic elements.'[39] In his memoir, *I Caught Crippen*, Metropolitan Police Inspector, Walter Dew, asserted that the district had 'a reputation for vice and villainy unequalled anywhere else in the British Isles'.

The attitude of the upper classes was not to help improve the area and the lives of those living in it, but either to pretend it did not exist, or get rid of the problem by wiping the district out. Social reformer, the Reverend Samuel Barnett, had asked for Flower and Dean Street to be demolished under the Artisans and Labourers Act, as a 'criminal slum'.[40] In 1883 he had got his wish when 13,000 people from the street were made homeless. They included many single or (like Polly), separated women who managed to afford the higher rents elsewhere by offering sex for money.

In spite of Barnett's demolition programme, the East End continued to be synonymous with deprivation and vice. In 1902, when undercover reporter, Jack London, asked for information about the area from the driver of his hansom cab, the reply came back: 'It is over there, somewhere'. People knew nothing about the district, he said. They merely 'waved their hands vaguely in the direction where the sun on rare occasions may be seen to rise'.[41]

They were not speaking metaphorically: visibility in the East End was literally poor, for there were few gaslights, and those there were gave out only smudges of illumination. When it was foggy, which was often the case, visibility was much worse. Francis Russell, son of former Prime Minister John Russell, had written in 1880 that:

> A London fog is brown, reddish-yellow, or greenish... has a smoky, or sulphurous smell... and produces, when thick, a choking sensation.... A white cloth spread out on the ground rapidly turns dirty, and particles of soot attach themselves to every exposed object.

When there was an especially thick fog – and the 1880s was proving the worst decade for fogs there had ever been – gaslamps were kept on throughout the day. Even then you would need a link-boy carrying a flaming torch to see you through the darkness.[42] Any would-be attacker had no trouble creeping up behind their victims, or standing in an alley ready to waylay them, without being seen.

Buying poor quality secondhand clothes so as to blend in with the locals, Jack London roamed around the East End a decade or so after the Ripper murders. He described it as 'one unending slum', inhabited by close to half a million miserable creatures. It presented a pitiful spectacle. The area was filled with 'a new and different race of people, short of stature, and of wretched or beer-sodden appearance'. There were long stretches of 'bricks and misery' and 'slimy pavements'. In the 'screaming streets' it was commonplace for drunken women to fight. He began to mix with men of 'deadly inertia', whose only demand was an evening pipe of tobacco and their regular 'arf an' arf' to drink. When he crossed the road, wearing his old clothes, he had to take greater care than usual not to be knocked down because '[his] life had cheapened'.[43]

As for the women of Whitechapel, there were hundreds in a similar predicament to Polly's. Their lives had not merely altered but depreciated, both in their own eyes and in those of the authorities. Their dreams shattered, their main concern was to survive each day, each hour.

Almost half the inhabitants had no home of their own. Instead they 'dossed', like Polly would, in one of the many common lodging-houses, where a bed could be had for fourpence – or threepence if you shared it. In some, you could get away with paying a mere twopence, provided you were prepared to sit on a bench and lean against a rope: It was called a 'twopenny hangover'. Failing that, you had to stay out at night and 'carry the banner', as it was known. No matter how sick or old, lodgers had to leave by ten o'clock every morning, pouring out into the congested streets, where carriages passed four abreast, and drivers were so short of space that they had to park their carts sideways.

Hawkers and costermongers gathered on the north side of Whitechapel Road, selling anything from beds to boots, books to bloaters, tools to tulips. Stalls were crammed with apples and pears, vegetables and oysters. Working by the light of greasy oil burners, naphtha lamps, or a mere candle or two, the cries and patter of sellers could be heard past midnight, offering sheep's trotters, pea soup and hot pies; and there were plenty of customers, for much of Whitechapel's population was on the street at night. Vendors of quack medicines jostled for space with buskers and child acrobats, Indians selling scarves, beggars touting fruit or flowers, and hokey-pokey men selling what they called 'Italian' ice cream but which was no more Italian than Stoke Newington. Older Jewish street sellers fiercely competed with the more recent Irish traders.[44]

Gaunt and scruffy children sang ditties, or told jokes to raise a few pennies. Others collected cigar ends, or old bits of bread to soak in water, that their families would use to bulk out a dish of oatmeal. Their lives were precarious: fifty-five per cent of East End children died under five years old, compared with eighteen per cent in the more prosperous West End.[45] Even for children, job opportunities for males and females were unequal. Whereas poor boys might manage to earn a few pennies as market porters or labourers, all that girls could do was sell a few flowers, matches, or ultimately themselves.

While men queued at the gates of the West India Docks, and fought for a couple of hours' casual work unloading barrels or bags of sugar from ships, their women, dressed in cloth caps and aprons, tried to find work as poorly paid skivvies. Others took to sewing. But that would mean providing their own thread, needles and candles, and paying for heating. Their working hours would be unthinkable today. 'My usual time of work is from five in the morning till nine at night – winter and summer… But when there is press of business, I work earlier and later….', reported one seamstress. Wages were derisory: 'I clears about 2s 6d a week…. I know it's so little I can't get a rag to my back', she continued.[46]

Many women of Polly's age stood with baskets of firewood, cutlery, stationery and plated goods. Old women, who would never have the means to retire, could be seen wading knee-deep in piles of rubbish, scavenging for something of value. 'Pure-finders' collected dog turds and sold them to tanners who used them in the process of dressing leather. Some women openly begged on the streets. Their stories followed a familiar pattern: 'My husband is in bed with the fever'; 'I am a widow and have seven babies to feed.' Polly might have tried telling the story of her own life: it had been no less tough. But there was no knowing whether without anything to sell she would be able to survive.

Other women stood out in their garish outfits, and non-matching shawls, worn on top of mountains of clothes – everything they owned.

These 'loose', 'fallen' women, or 'harlots', sported nicknames such as 'Lushing Loo' and 'Swindling Sal'. Their cheap blue silk emulated that of a Victorian lady as they flaunted themselves in and around pubs, their faces haggard and pock-marked, their voices described as shrill: 'like sick owls'.[47]

Polly looked nothing like them, standing a slight five foot two inches tall in her rough brown Ulster coat with its big buttons. In the broken bit of looking glass she always carried with her, she observed how her once dark brown hair was turning grey. Although some people thought she looked younger, she was now over forty years old, like numerous other street prostitutes. Also like many of them, Polly's family had abandoned her mainly because of her drink problem.

Some of these women stood outside pubs, but that risked being arrested for loitering. Polly would never do this. Patrolling a beat, she dipped into hostelries for clients. She certainly had plenty to choose from: forty-eight pubs in a one-mile stretch between Commercial Street and Stepney Green. One of her favourites was a rough place called the *Frying Pan*, run by William Farrow on the corner of Brick Lane and Thrawl Street. She would have taken her pick-ups, many of them regulars, down the nearest dark alley or yard to have sex standing up and fully dressed, either in doorways, or braced against railings. In these murky conditions they would perhaps not notice her baggy eyes and her missing front teeth; just as her fellow prostitutes hoped that their swollen bellies and skin diseases would also go unobserved.

Only a year before Polly's arrival in Whitechapel, brewery-heir Frederick Charrington had spearheaded a campaign to rid the East End of prostitution. It was Charrington's opinion that prostitutes were either morally weak, or sexually insatiable nymphomaniacs – 'daughters of joy' who had 'violated their womanhood' for the price of a night's lodging. Their only hope of salvation, he told them, was to reform by going into a refuge, train as a factory worker, or become a servant in a respectable family. In his black book he noted down suspected brothels, music halls outside which prostitutes congregated, massage parlours, and so-called 'nursing homes', where 'nursing nymphs in flimsy clothing' ministered to the desires of elderly gentlemen. One after another he got them closed down.[48]

In this climate Polly could not openly solicit, for that would get her reported and arrested; instead she would most probably have thrown a stealthy glance, or uttered a mumbled word. Who cared about Mr Friggin' Charrington? It was none of his business how she came by a few coins, as long as she managed to earn enough to pay for her gin, and a bed for the night. Seeing a lighted lamp outside a 'kip-house' was a great relief for Polly because it was a sign that there was a bed available inside, provided she came up with fourpence. Even if this was in Thrawl Street – a street so dangerous that policemen were said to walk around in threes.

The night of 2 August 1888 she shared a room at a house run by Daniel Lewis at 18 Thrawl Street, Spitalfields, with three other women, and a bed with a woman who sometimes called herself Ellen Holland, at other times Jane Oram. Whatever her real name, she was hoping to get married, until she fell out with her sweetheart who had been supporting her. Ever since she had been reduced to earning pennies by picking up sailors at the docks.

Polly too could earn threepence or fourpence a trick – from workers at Spitalfields Market, or out-of-town traders; perhaps even from West End gentlemen on a 'slumming' excursion. But she planned only to do so until things improved, and she could find regular work. Many women like her drifted in and out of prostitution – it was not a job they intended doing for life. Doctor and writer William Acton referred to it as 'oscillatory prostitution', a 'transitory state', seeing as 'by far the larger number of women who have resorted to prostitution for a livelihood, return sooner or later to a more or less regular course of life'.[49] When census enumerators asked them what they did for a living, they would say: dressmaker, servant, laundry maid, charwoman, housekeeper, seamstress, stay-maker, cap or bonnet-maker, or other respectable jobs. In reality, they were none of these, for there was no work to be had. Rather than enter a workhouse – which would mean separation from their children – they chose, from a series of unpalatable options, to walk the streets.

From 24–30 August 1888 we know Polly had a bed at the 'White House', 56 Flower and Dean Street, Spitalfields, next door to Cooney's, a well-known lodging-house. The place was surrounded by streets that shared chilling nicknames such as Blood Alley, Frying Pan Alley, Shovel Alley, and Do-as-you-please street.[50] All had become warrens for the very poor. Groups of young lads and girls – many of them thieves – hung around in the middle of the road. Women who were unable to afford a bed would congregate in a shed on Dorset Street to eat bread and butter, and drink cans of beer; while 'fourpenny knee tremblers' with painted faces took their clients into one of the street's many murky corners for sex.[51]

Only sixteen feet wide and narrowing to only ten feet at either end, Flower and Dean Street, which was to be Polly's home for a week, was described by one local newspaper as being 'associated in most people's minds with vice, immorality and crime in their most hideous shapes… there is no street in any part of the Metropolis that has for its inhabitants a like number of the dangerous class'.[52]

The thoroughfare provided a rookery for thieves, especially men who committed violent robberies. Knife assaults were all too common. When philanthropist and social reformer, Dr Thomas Barnardo, visited the street as part of his mission to save homeless children from a life of crime, a group of roughs robbed him not only of his money but also his hat, coat, watch and chain.

The main buildings were very tall: three storeys of smoke-blackened brick and timber, some jutting out at first and second floors. The original residents had possessed back gardens, but these had been cut up to form a multitude of dark courts and alleys. Many houses did not even have numbers, and were identified by the colour of their lamps outside: red, blue, and, in the case of No. 56, white.

What marked off Flower and Dean Street was the great number of almost entirely unregulated common lodging-houses, thirty-one in all, which provided nightly accommodation for almost one thousand men and women – some of London's very poorest inhabitants, who formed a mobile population of thieves, beggars and prostitutes.

At the White House beds generally cost fourpence a night. Those who could afford to do so paid a week in advance and that way got Sunday night free. Rising from their straw mattresses each morning, lodgers ate breakfast in a basement kitchen, and washed under a pump in the yard. They had no idea where the pennies they needed for their bed the next night would come from. In any case, before darkness arrived they would first need to survive another day in the East End.

James Smith, the owner of the house, allowed men and women to sleep together in the dormitories, without asking to see a marriage certificate. Double beds were available at a cost of eightpence for prostitutes and their clients, partitioned off by a hoarding that often did not reach the floor or ceiling. At least if any of their punters got rough they could call upon one another, or the men, to come to their rescue.

One or two nights Polly may have stayed in a lodging-house run by George and Mary Cushway at No. 9 Leman Street. Their daughter had married William Nichols's cousin, and Polly knew they would always find a bed for her at a cheap rate.

On 30 August, having given her appearance a quick check over in her glass, Polly left No.56 and made off towards Whitechapel Road, where one witness noticed her walking alone at around 11.30 p.m.

Next morning, at 12.30 a.m., she was observed leaving the *Frying Pan.*

Slightly tipsy, she was seen making for her doss in Flower and Dean Street at 1.20 a.m. But the deputy turned her away because she could not pay fourpence for her bed. As she went, she laughed: 'I'll soon get my doss money – see what a jolly bonnet I've got now!' Polly was proudly sporting a little black bonnet that nobody had seen before.

An hour later, at the corner of Osborne Street and Brick Lane, she met her room mate, Ellen Holland, who was returning from watching a great fire in one of the huge brandy and gin warehouses down at Ratcliff Dock on the South Quay. When she saw Polly leaning against the wall outside a grocer's shop, drunk, she went over to her and they spoke for seven or eight minutes until the church clock struck half past two. Polly was in very good spirits on account of the gin she had been drinking.

Her friend tried to get her to return to the doss-house but she said she hadn't got any money: 'I've had my lodging money three times today and I've spent it' at the *Frying Pan*, or the *The Ten Bells*: 'I won't be long before I'm back!'

She told Ellen that she had asked the landlord to save her a bed.

With that, Polly staggered off down Whitechapel Road, hoping to earn the fourpence she needed. Her steel-tipped heels clattered on the stones for a bit as she headed in the direction of Buck's Row; then there was nothing, silence.

Buck's Row was 'a narrow, cobbled, mean street' behind Whitechapel underground station, lined on one side by 'shabby little houses of two storeys', on the other by the grim silhouette of the board school. The high, blackened walls of warehouses and Smith & Co.'s distillery shadowed the dirty street in a deep gloom. A pavement, no more than three feet wide, separated those on foot from the road, which can only have measured twenty feet from one wall to the other.[53]

At 3.45 a.m. PC John Neil was summoned to Buck's Row by two labourers who told him that a woman lay either drunk or dead in a gateway. His 'bull's eye' lantern gave off very little light, but it was sufficient to glimpse blood oozing from the woman's throat.

Neil sent his fellow officer, PC John Thain, to fetch Dr Rees Ralph Llewellyn and the 'ambulance' – a heavy, cumbersome handcart, used for removing drunks.

The doctor arrived soon after 4 a.m. By then, PC Jonas Mizen was also on the scene, and workmen from the surrounding warehouses and slaughtermen from Barber's Yard, Winthrop Street, had gathered around to gawp.

Llewellyn concluded that the woman's throat had been cut from ear to ear with a long-bladed knife. As her legs were still warm, it was his opinion she had not been dead more than half an hour. He ordered that she be taken to the Whitechapel Mortuary in Old Montague Street, next to Whitechapel Workhouse. Reached by gates in Eagle Place, the building was little more than a shed, and was completely inadequate for conducting a post-mortem.

Ignoring instructions not to do so, mortuary workers Robert Mann and James Hatfield stripped and washed Polly's body. While they were

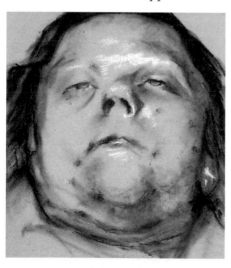

about their task, a local resident washed away the congealed blood from the cobblestones by the gateway in Buck's Row.

A cursory examination by Inspector John Spratling at the mortuary revealed a two-inch wound to Polly's throat. The lower part of her abdomen was completely ripped open and her bowels were protruding. A four-inch incision had been made below her left ear, while an eight-inch gash encircled her throat, completely severing the tissues down to her spine.

Mortuary photograph of Mary Ann Nichols. (Wikimedia Commons)

Her hands were bruised and showed evidence of a struggle. Two front teeth had been knocked out, and there was bruising to both cheeks.

In Polly's pocket was found a piece of comb, her looking glass, and a plain handkerchief; but it was the crucial discovery of the mark 'Lambeth Workhouse P.R.' on one of the two petticoats she was wearing that led the police to Mrs Scorer and subsequently to Mary Ann Monk, Polly's fellow inmates at the workhouse. Mrs Scorer's husband, James, appeared on her behalf, though he only knew Polly by sight and could not identify her with any certainty.

But when Mary Ann Monk arrived at 7.30 p.m. she at once recognised her friend in her brown Ulster coat, claiming that she had seen her only the evening previously going into a pub in the New Kent Road. Furthermore, she was able to help the police trace her husband, her father, and her son Edward John.

William Nichols, who lived with Rosetta Walls across the river in Coburg Road, Southwark, arrived later that evening, dressed in a suit and carrying an umbrella. Some eight years had passed since he and Polly had lived together. His earlier feelings of anger, disgust, and humiliation had given way to a numb coldness.

Nichols was shown Polly's body. Her brown eyes lacked their usual lustre, and her complexion was dark. It was some while before he could muster any words at all: 'Seeing you as you are now', he said eventually, 'I forgive you for what you have done to me.'

Mary Ann Nichols's death certificate. (Public domain)

Emerging, pale and shaking, he added: 'Well, there is no mistake about it. It has come to a sad end at last.'

* * *

An inquest into her death opened on Saturday 1 September at the Working Lads' Institute in Whitechapel Road. The first witness to be called was her father, who had not seen Polly for three years. Edward Walker said that her drinking had caused him and his daughter to argue but that he did not throw her out. He had a home for her but she had chosen to leave him in order to 'better herself'. He had no idea that she had been living in the East End, and rejected any suggestion that she was 'fast'.

The inquest established that the cause of death was: 'Violent syncope from loss of blood from wounds in neck and abdomen inflicted by some sharp instrument', and the autopsy report from Dr Rees Ralph Llewellyn referred to her killer's dexterity, as well as considerable savagery, with the knife. Yet no one had seen or heard anything, not even the occupants of the cottages by the gates near where Polly had been found.

On Thursday 6 September 1888, Polly was taken in a polished elm coffin to the City of London Cemetery, Ilford, where she was buried.[54] Many of the houses along the route of the procession had their blinds down, and police were stationed every few yards along Baker's Row and past the corner of Buck's Row.

Her father and her son, Edward John Nichols, together with two more of Polly's children, attended her funeral. Although he paid for the occasion, William Nichols was conspicuously absent.[55]

* * *

In June 1894, six years after Polly's murder, William Nichols, now aged fifty, married thirty-seven-year-old Rosetta Walls.[56]

Chapter 2

Annie Chapman
('Dark Annie')

When Eliza Anne Smith – or Annie as she became known – was born in a small terraced house in Paddington, West London, on 8 September 1841, the character of the district had already begun to change. Once known as Paddington Green, industrialisation was making it more of a smoky grey. Harrow Road, the street in which she lived, had become a busy and congested thoroughfare into central London,[1] and an abundance of workers' houses now packed its side streets. Yet there were still traces of what had been a once salubrious area, in the grand garden squares and elegant cream-stuccoed terraces that housed the 'well-to-do' and 'comfortable' classes[2], only a few streets away from Annie's home, close to the Regent's Canal.

Annie's father, George, a burly, six-foot-tall man, served in the 2nd Life Guards, which formed part of Queen Victoria's Household Cavalry. Her mother, Ruth Chapman, came locally from Market Street. Both were excessive drinkers or, as people would say in those days, 'habitual drunkards'. Deemed unable to control their appetite for alcohol, they were regarded no more highly than lunatics, who also lacked willpower over their whimsical behaviour, and could not hold down a job.

On 22 February 1842, nearly six months after Annie was born, her parents married at St James's Church, Westbourne Terrace. The Victorians placed great importance on children being born to married couples, and to wed, as Ruth and George were doing, after the birth of a child was not 'respectable', and broke the social conventions of the day. Their notorious drinking habits would have underlined their disrespect towards authority, and spelt ruin for their family.

Many unmarried mothers at this time were unable to support their babies, and had to hand them over to foundling hospitals. But George Smith stood by his young woman, did the honourable thing and married her.

Although never involved in active military service, Trooper Smith was responsible for helping protect Queen Victoria and the royal family at their London residences, including St James's Palace, Kensington Palace and Buckingham Palace. This entailed transfers from one barracks to another: from Hyde Park, to Kensington, Upper Albany Street, Regent's Park and back again to Hyde Park. It was there that a sister, Emily Latitia Smith, was born at 4 Rutland Terrace in November 1844; she was a toddler when the family went to live nearby at 3 Montpelier Place, a neat Georgian yellow-brick terraced house with spearheaded iron railings and an ornate, fan-shaped window above the front door.

As they grew up, the sisters turned out to be complete opposites, and never hit it off. Whereas Emily Latitia was shy and quiet, planned ahead, and was keen to obey the rules, Annie was outgoing, loud, fickle and headstrong, prepared to take chances. She wasn't in the least bit interested in conforming to people's ideas about how a young girl should behave.

In April 1856, when she was fourteen years old – grown-up in those days – another sister, Georgina, was born. By this time, her father was working some twenty-five miles away at the Victoria Barracks in Windsor, a sleepy medieval town in Berkshire, which had been launched into the modern era by the arrival of the railway, and was now growing rapidly.

The Smiths lived immediately beneath Windsor Castle in Clewer New Town. Their house, 12 Keppel Terrace, was one of thirteen cottages strung out along St Leonard's Road – 'desirable residences' for genteel families in a respectable neighbourhood, to cite a newspaper advertisement from the time.[3] The family occupied three floors, each with two rooms, and a basement. On the first floor at the front was a balcony, and the rear offered them fine views over St Leonard's Hill and the River Thames.

A third sister, Mirium Ruth, arrived in 1858. As she grew up, Annie was to find her stiff and formal, a prude, and she got on no better with her than with her other sisters.

By 1861 the family of six had returned to London where a brother, Fountain Hamilton, was born at 6 Middle Row North, Knightsbridge, in February.[4] Barely had the child taken his first steps, when Annie's father was moved back to Windsor. Queen Victoria was residing more and more here, following Prince Albert's untimely death from fever at the age of forty-two. The family, with the exception of Annie, their eldest child, uprooted again and returned to Clewer, this time settling further along Keppel Terrace at No. 7.

Annie is believed to have stayed in London and found work as a domestic servant in the West End. It is possible that she was the Annie Smith recorded in the 1861 census, living with another servant at 2 Duke Street, close to Oxford Street, with its busy department stores, street traders, and prostitutes.

By then, her father had retired from the army, and was working as a gentleman's manservant to supplement his tiny pension. After a lengthy military career, this sudden change in circumstances would appear to have unnerved him and he became deeply unhappy. During a bout of depression in 1864 he took his own life by cutting his throat.

His sudden death came as a terrible shock, and brought with it serious money problems for the family. Ruth immediately took the children back to London, where a friend offered them free lodging at No. 29 Montpelier Place, Knightsbridge. They just had to get on with their lives as best they could, without complaining, or wallowing in self-pity.

* * *

Several years earlier, while living in Windsor, Annie had got to know John Chapman. A relative on her mother's side of the family, he had moved to Berkshire from Newmarket in Suffolk. Chapman was three years younger than her, and cut a dashing figure with his light beard, curly hair and tailcoat. He had obtained work as a valet for a Windsor nobleman – a respectable position, considerably above that of stablehand or groom.

As part of his responsibilities, Chapman was entrusted with his master's keys. These included the key to a well-stocked drinks cabinet containing wines and spirits. John enjoyed a tipple, and Annie also would look forward to a glass or two when she came to see him. Her favourite liquor was rum, and she quickly developed a taste for it.

When she moved to London in 1861, John Chapman continued to visit her and they would go walking in the parks, as young couples did.

During one of these visits to London he asked her to become his wife. She accepted.

Annie and John
Chapman *c.*1869,
the year of
their marriage.
(Chapman family/
Neal Shelden)

On 1 May 1869, at All Saints Church, Ennismore Gardens in Kensington,[5] John Chapman married Annie Smith, an attractive twenty-seven year-old woman with dark brown wavy hair and sparkling blue eyes.

Seeing as there was regular employment for valets in London, their future seemed rosy and they could think about having a family. After a few months living with Ruth at Montpelier Place, in 1870 the couple moved to their first married home at 1 Brook Mews, Bayswater, where a daughter, Emily Ruth Jane, was born on 25 June.

With a little one to feed, it became more difficult to manage the rent, especially as Annie was spending some of John's allowance on rum. The following year the couple returned to live with her mother.

After several stillborn babies, Annie gave birth to a second daughter. Annie Georgina Chapman was to lead a colourful life, some sources claiming that she attended a college in France, and travelled with a circus; though her descendants maintain she was employed as a servant to a court dresser[6].

By this time, John was working for a nobleman in one of London's most exclusive thoroughfares, Bond Street in Mayfair, home to some of the city's most fashionable and expensive shops, and frequented by equally wealthy ladies and gentlemen. In the Burlington Arcade, an elegant shopping mall running between Bond Street and Piccadilly, one could purchase glittering jewellery, soft cashmere, luxurious chocolates – and sex. Between three and five every afternoon, the 'better class' of prostitutes would gather there to find clients – a country farmer on a trip to the city, or an elderly man with silver hair – and take them to rooms they rented above nearby shops.

John and Annie had found a place to stay a few streets away at 17 South Bruton Mews, which looked out on Berkeley Square, with its well-tended lawn, plane trees and ornamental fountain. They were in illustrious company: a number of famous residents had occupied houses in that square, including the historian, writer and politician, Horace Walpole; the British military commander, Robert Clive of India; and former Prime Minister, George Canning.

With regular work and a home in opulent surroundings, all appeared to be going well for them. But it was not to last. Something Annie did – maybe she pawned the nobleman's fine clothes, or more likely, stole a bottle of rum – got John the sack.

News of his dismissal was openly condemned by her brother and sisters. Their strict moral principles always kept them on the straight and narrow, and all led steady lives. Fountain had secured a job as a printer's warehouseman, and was living at home with his mother so that he could save up enough to marry his girl. Annie's sisters, Emily Latitia, Georgina and Mirium Ruth, all dressmakers living nearby, had become religious converts, and worshipped regularly at St Michael and All Angels Church in Star Street, Paddington.

Horrified by their parents' heavy drinking, they had joined the temperance movement, which had begun in the US and crossed the Atlantic to Britain around 1830. It was becoming increasingly popular among the middle classes who were appalled by the sight of drunks lying unconscious in London's streets.

Contemporaries were divided about the causes of drunkenness. Some considered it a moral illness that preyed on weak-minded individuals; others thought of it as a disease of the nervous system. While some believed that the condition was inherited, others thought it took root in those with an 'acutely sensitive temperament'.

One society set up to cure habitual drunkards was in no doubt how addiction began:

> The frequent depression produced by any extra mental or physical strain, or the disappointments and trials of life, to which such persons are painfully susceptible, prompt them to resort to stimulants for sustentation and comfort.

It was also aware of the vicious circle that drunkards got themselves caught up in, and how drinking 'demands still further supplies of stimulants' that created an 'irresistible drink-craving', impossible to extricate oneself from without help.[7]

Concerned that 'a once-great nation was floating to its ruin on a sea of alcohol', as one historian puts it,[8] reformers began to mobilise. Temperance societies were set up in Britain, which sought to address the problem of alcoholism – not through legislation but by persuading people to take an 'abstinence pledge'.

Meeting in temperance halls and institutes, members would publish and circulate moral pamphlets that could be read in their libraries, where tea, ginger beer, lemonade and peppermint water were the only drinks available for those who were thirsty.

Gaining support for their views from the nonconformist churches, and later from the Church of England and the middle classes, they argued that people who over-indulged in alcohol risked crossing 'rickety bridges', and would have to negotiate a lifetime of 'slippery slopes'.

At first, the temperance societies had no issue with people drinking beer or wine, provided this was carried out 'in moderation'. But a single glass of a spirit, such as gin, available for a few pennies at a public house, was destined to lead to a person's ruin, and to their children becoming thieves and prostitutes. Some teetotallers went further and favoured people taking the 'long pledge' by also promising not to offer alcohol to others.

With their parents' drinking excesses still fresh in their memory, Annie's brother and sisters took to heart what the local society preached about the dangers of drink. Annie, on the other hand, was reluctant to get involved with a group of do-gooders, and it took much coaxing by her siblings before she agreed to join them in signing a pledge, attending a ceremony and going up to accept a certificate that bore the mottos 'Touch Not, Taste Not, Handle Not' along the bottom edge.

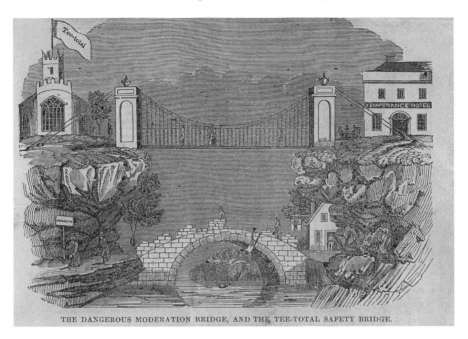

THE DANGEROUS MODERATION BRIDGE, AND THE TEE-TOTAL SAFETY BRIDGE.

The temperance societies compared over-indulgence in alcohol to crossing a rickety bridge. (Temperance Picture Gallery)

Many contemporaries were sceptical about what temperance societies could expect to achieve. 'The temperance advocates may preach their hearts out over the evils of drink', wrote Jack London, 'but until the evils that cause people to drink are abolished, drink and its evils will remain'.[9]

In practice, drinking in Britain remained as popular as ever. An increasing number of women began to drink, and they had no shame about going into pubs to take a nip. Indeed, they were welcomed inside and were a common sight in London, observed the researcher Charles Booth. Some pubs even had ladies' saloons – and women regularly got drunk on spirits, downing them as if they were drinking tea.[10]

For Annie, that spirit was rum. As her craving grew, it became impossible for her to get through the day without it. A mere drop gave her a lift. Merely because she had a certificate to say she was an abstainer, what of it? Her pledge had no standing in law. It wasn't as if by going back on her word she were committing a crime.

Exasperated by his wife's drinking problem, John suggested she spend time in a home for the intemperate. This was a voluntary retreat, or refuge, for 'inebriates' who were addicted to alcoholic drinks. There they would be kept in quarantine for their own safety, as well as that of other people. Sometime in 1877, when he offered to pay for her treatment, board and lodging, Annie agreed to go in.

Inside these refuges, which were soon to become more numerous[11], attempts were made to cure drunkenness. The home provided Annie with all necessary treatments, including vapour baths and massages, and a diet of vegetables and tonics made from strychnine, quinine and coca bark, that aimed to restore 'nerve power'. As it was thought impossible to make a moderate drinker of any drunkard who had lost their self-control, total abstinence was the only remedy, and all intoxicating stimulants were banned. The behaviour of patients also needed managing, their conversation with others monitored, and their reading material and mail checked, to stop them becoming susceptible to bad influences.

To occupy her time doing something worthwhile, she learned how to make little baskets and cut out artificial flowers. She preferred to crochet antimacassars, pieces of cloth that were placed over the headrests and arms of chairs to protect them from grease and dirt.

The months passed. Summer gave way to autumn, and Christmas found Annie still at the refuge, receiving treatment.

* * *

All this while John kept in touch with his friends in Windsor by letter, and in 1878 these connections paid off when he was told there was a situation available for him as a coachman, or chauffeur – a prestigious position in the hierarchy of servants within a large household.

His new employer was Josiah Weeks, a farm bailiff who worked at St Leonard's Hill on land owned by Sir Francis Tress Barry. A former British Vice-Consul in Spain, Barry had turned his back on a diplomatic career to become a businessman, and had amassed a fortune from copper mines in Portugal. Most of his time he spent, not in Windsor, but on his Caithness estate in Scotland.[12] During these periods Weeks was in charge, and John Chapman had the responsibility of transporting him in style from place to place. When Weeks was not travelling around, the coachman still needed to be present in order to project an image of the Barry family's considerable wealth and status within the community.

While Annie continued in London for a full year with treatment to break her addiction, her husband and daughters lodged over the stables at St Leonard's Hill Mansion, and were provided with a nanny called Caroline Aylesbury.

One of Annie's sisters paid for Annie Georgina to attend a classy finishing school for ladies in Windsor, where she learned to speak French, play the piano, and was trained in good posture or deportment, so as to make her a fitting companion for a future husband when they travelled.

Most of Caroline Aylesbury's time was spent tending to Emily Ruth Jane, who suffered epileptic fits. The early Victorians had little understanding of the causes of this condition: even a number of doctors believed it was caused by masturbation; and ignorance was still worse among the general public. Many people who witnessed seizures were terrified, thinking they were contagious, or a sign of being 'possessed' by the Devil. Epileptics were often made fun of as freaks, and confined to lunatic asylums, epileptic colonies, and hospitals for the paralysed. Physicians frequently declared that epileptics should not be permitted to marry because their children would inherit their affliction.[13]

In London the outlook for Annie's condition was brighter, and when her course of treatment was complete, she left the refuge and returned to live with her husband and children in Berkshire – seemingly a changed and sober woman.

However, those living on Sir Francis Tress Barry's estate did not welcome her back, being suspicious that she had not really reformed. Their fears were not unfounded. According to one story, Annie's drinking habits suddenly returned when she kissed her husband goodbye as he was going to work one morning. John had just downed a hot whisky to relieve a cold, and the taste of the liquor on his lips was too much of a temptation for Annie. Within an hour she had reverted to her old self: a 'drunken, mad woman'.

Although she was carrying their child, John told her she must leave, that he risked losing his position if she remained.

Annie went to stay with a friend in the village of Water Oakley, outside Windsor.

On 21 November 1880 a son, John Alfred, was born. It was soon clear that something was wrong, and a physician confirmed that the boy was partially paralysed. The news devastated Annie. She took the boy to

London and placed him in a specialist hospital[14], where patients received 'humane and skilled investigation, management, and treatment', including hot and cold plunge baths, and electrotherapy. It was all useless, and when the boy returned, many who knew Annie viewed John Alfred with a mixture of pity, discomfort and fear. Some thought that as he grew up, he might start lashing out.

When Emily died on 26 November 1882 – not from epilepsy but from meningitis – Mirium blamed her death, together with John Alfred's paralysis, and Annie's numerous stillborn babies, on her sister going back on her abstinence pledge and taking to the bottle again.

Yet it was drink that probably helped her forget her troubles. It would have given her some respite in the evenings, before her problems began all over again when the sun rose next day.

By 1884 her addiction had become worse than ever, and the whole of her weekly allowance went on rum, leaving her nothing left for food and clothes. John had done all he could for her. Unable to tolerate the situation any longer, he insisted that she leave, and swore that he would never take her back.

Annie would not go. Only when Sir Francis Tress Barry refused to allow her to remain on his estate was she forced to leave. For weeks afterwards she was seen wandering the Berkshire countryside, dressed in a shabby skirt and filthy boots.

Eventually she gave up and returned to London, but not to Paddington where they had once lived. She had neither the money nor the contacts to find lodging there. Instead she made her way east, towards Whitechapel, where people said she could find cheap accommodation in one of the numerous common lodging-houses, the doors of which were always open to casual workers who might rent a bed there by the night. Perhaps she could keep jolly company around a big kitchen fire, eat kippers and bread and butter, and drink tea. It wouldn't be so bad.

Once the East End had been a prosperous area, noted for its silk industry. But during the 1880s, more and more people poured into London, arriving at the docks after long journeys at sea. They included persecuted Jewish refugees fleeing Poland and Russia – boot-makers, tailors, and each year some one thousand unaccompanied women, much like Annie, all hoping for a brighter future.

In practice, many were robbed of their belongings at the docks, or tricked into buying tickets for non-existent forward passages to America, where they were promised work and somewhere to live. They found themselves instead huddled together in overcrowded tenements down dark alleys where single rooms often housed an extended family, from tiny babies to aged grandparents, all eking out an existence, ever on the brink of starvation.

In his survey of 1886–1903, Charles Booth estimated that twenty-two per cent of the population lived on the poverty line; whilst thirteen per cent struggled against conditions in which 'decent life was not imaginable'.[15] American senator W.C. Preston remembered visiting a house where the cellar was occupied by a father, mother, three children and four pigs. In another room, a man lay ill with smallpox and the children ran around naked and dirty. One underground kitchen was occupied by seven people, together with the corpse of a child that the family could not afford to bury.[16]

Of all the districts, it was Whitechapel that had the capital's worst slums, severest overcrowding and highest death rates, with disease and hunger claiming the lives of one in four children before they reached one year old. The area's common lodging (or 'doss' -) houses were breeding grounds for infection and disease. A subterranean kitchen, swarming with cockroaches and black beetles, would double up as a sitting room, while above were crammed several fetid dormitories. As often as not, conditions were even worse than those to be found in the casual ward of a workhouse. There were no fireplaces in the dormitories, so in winter lodgers would shiver in the cold. Sheets were only changed once a month, and the rows of beds – squeezed in across the floor and nicknamed 'coffin beds' – wriggled with vermin.

Even these pitiful quarters were only available at night. During the daylight hours, residents had to leave the premises, no matter how sick or old they were, and whatever the weather. All they could do was doze in doorways, in parks, or on the street, until the police chased them away.

This was the world Annie was about to enter – home to the 'wicked', 'idle' and 'good-for-nothing' poor – where boys and girls had to play on the street or in filthy courtyards until their mothers and fathers returned from the pub at midnight or one o'clock in the morning.

Like so many others, she had arrived in the East End without money of her own. From time to time, her husband sent her payments of ten shillings by postal order, which she could cash at the local post office on Commercial Street. But with no regular income, she became desperate.

On 10 October 1885 a woman by the name of Annie Chapman was charged at the Thames Magistrates' Court with stealing a hammer and was fined one pound, or given fourteen days in prison. If this was indeed Annie, she presumably had to accept fourteen days inside.

Afterwards she returned to Whitechapel, where those who knew her described her as a very respectable, quiet but sociable woman, who never used bad language, was clever and well educated, and often read in her leisure time. Determined to make a living from her own labour, she resumed her crochet, and would walk to Stratford East (today's West Ham) to hawk it – some three miles each way.[17] The area was growing fast, with factories and thousands of houses being built for the families of professional men and clerks who worked in London. Annie no doubt reckoned she could sell them handmade wicker baskets, and simple artificial flowers made from dyed paper for their wives' dresses and bonnets – for in those days no woman would leave home without an attractively decorated hat. To protect their armchairs from well-oiled hair, she could offer her crocheted antimacassars, which she had made using scraps of cloth and old bits of wool.

When this failed, she would go to Whitechapel and Spitalfields and live off her men friends. Although jobs for women were few and far between, there were often opportunities for men as porters or general labourers. Ted Stanley, ('the pensioner'), who won her over with tales of how he had served as a soldier in the Essex Regiment, worked as a bricklayer's mate; while another friend, John (or 'Jack') Sievey, who earned Annie the nickname 'Dark Annie Sievey', made wire sieves for a living.

* * *

In Clewer that same summer, 1886, John Chapman resigned his job as coachman due to ill health, and went to live in New Windsor. Although he had been paying into a sickness club to provide for hard times such as these, his benefit would not stretch to paying Annie her weekly allowance.

In the autumn, John's brother, who lived in Whitechapel, told Annie that her husband had become worse. Unable to afford the fare by stagecoach or train, she walked all the way to Windsor, along the Thames by way of Richmond, sleeping in parks at night. It was a journey close on seventy miles there and back.

On Christmas Day she received news that John had died. His death was attributed to cirrhosis of the liver, brought about by drinking too much alcohol over the course of many years. He was forty-two years old.

Her friend, Amelia Palmer, who worked as a charwoman, said that Annie wept when she heard of John's death. She felt guilty that she had not been to see him again during the last two months. It was a terribly long walk but she should have made the effort to go.

Annie would never be the same person again. 'Since the death of her husband', said Palmer, she seemed to have given away all together'.

If matters were not bad enough, her friend Jack Sievey moved to Notting Hill in West London shortly afterwards.

Annie could not help thinking that she was being punished.

In order to earn a few pennies to buy a drink and a roof over her head, she now turned to selling herself.

At forty-five she had to compete for clients with girls who were half her age; but at least, unlike them, her years prevented her from conceiving a child.

Her night's work over, she would return to her digs at Crossingham's, 35 Dorset Street. Due to the large number of common lodging-houses

Crossingham's lodging-house, Dorset Street, on the corner of Little Paternoster Row, Whitechapel. It was demolished along with the entire north side of Dorset Street in 1928. (*Lloyds Weekly Newspaper* 2 June 1901)

Saturday night in Whitechapel: an illustration from Pictorial World, October 18th, 1883.

A lodging-house in Dorset Street, possibly Crossingham's. (*Pictorial World*, 18 October 1883)

that ran from one end to the other, locals called it 'Dosset Street'. It was home to the rough, criminal class, a place where you were all too likely to be attacked and robbed.

Managed by Timothy Donovan, a violent man by some accounts, Crossingham's accommodated on its four floors and in its basement about 300 lodgers, even though it was licensed to house only 114 men and women. Lodgers were herded in like cattle: 'The glimpses of life in these dens', commented Coroner Wynne Baxter, 'make us feel that there is much in the nineteenth century civilisation of which we have small reason to be proud'.[18]

Ted Stanley came down from Windsor, and he and Annie spent many a weekend together at Crossingham's. On several occasions he also paid the cost of a bed for Eliza Cooper, another of his fancy women. But he expected Annie to stay faithful to him, telling Donovan that if she showed up at Crossingham's with another man he should turn her away.

* * *

Towards the end of August 1888, Annie came across her brother, Fountain, on Commercial Road. He had done well for himself: the former printer's warehouseman had become a stationer, lived in fashionable Knightsbridge, and could now support a wife. Annie was reluctant to tell him where she was living, only that she was hard up. Fishing into his pocket, he produced two shillings and placed them in her palm.

Ted Stanley returned to the area on 1 September, and was on his way to Spitalfields Market when he met Annie at the corner of Commercial Street and Paternoster Row, where a blind man was playing a hurdy-gurdy, and women with baskets were selling passers-by snacks of jellied eels.

The following evening he saw Annie again at the 'Ringers', the nickname for *The Britannia* pub at the corner of Dorset Street and Commercial Street, which was run by Mr and Mrs Ringer. She was in the company of a man called 'Harry the Hawker' and Eliza Cooper, her rival for Ted's affections. According to Cooper, Annie was wearing three brass rings on the middle finger of her left hand.

Harry was drunk when a quarrel broke out, either over a florin (two shilling piece) that Annie claimed she saw Cooper stealing from

The Britannia, Dorset Street, known as the 'Ringers', where Annie Chapman often drank. (Casebook: Jack the Ripper – The Pubs of Whitechapel)

him and replacing with a halfpenny; or possibly over a piece of soap that Annie had not returned. Cooper struck Annie, leaving her with a black eye and a bruised chest.

The following day when she saw Amelia Palmer, Annie had no bonnet on and complained of feeling ill. Palmer said that Annie certainly looked pale and unwell.

'How did you get that?' she asked, noticing the bruise on Annie's right temple.

Annie opened her dress: 'Yes, look at my chest...' Then, in the next breath: 'If I can get a pair of boots from my sister I shall go hop-picking'.[19]

They parted company. Amelia went off charring. Since her husband's accident at the docks, the Palmers had to rely on his small army pension. Any extra pennies she could earn were always welcome.

No hop-picking boots had been forthcoming when Palmer met Annie again next day near Christ's Church, Spitalfields, where men, women and children, all dressed in rags, lay huddled on benches. Annie told her she was still feeling unwell, and that she would rest for a day or two in a 'spike' – the nickname for the casual ward of a workhouse. She explained how she had had nothing to eat or drink that day, not even a cup of tea, and Palmer gave her twopence, begging her not to spend it on rum.

To stand a chance of securing a bed for the night meant queuing up outside a workhouse from early afternoon. In the evening of 5 September, after a long wait outside the doors, Annie was admitted to Whitechapel Workhouse, where she was given a cold bath and a bowl of skilly – a thin porridge made from oatmeal and hot water.

Next morning, before she was allowed to leave, she was assigned jobs scrubbing, cleaning and mending ships' ropes, or 'picking oakum', as it was known.

At 5 p.m. on 7 September Amelia Palmer saw Annie again not far from her own lodging-house at 35 Dorset Street where she had stayed, off and on, for the last three years. This time she was sober. 'Are you going to Stratford?' she asked her, knowing that she plied her trade there.

Annie answered that she felt too ill at present to do anything.

Her friend encouraged her to be strong.

Eventually she rallied: 'It's no use my giving way.... I must pull myself together and go out and get some money or I shall have no lodgings'.

Whitechapel Workhouse, Vallance Road. (Jack London *The People of the Abyss,* 1903)

At 11.30 p.m. Annie returned to Crossingham's after several days' absence. It was a chilly evening, and she sat by the kitchen fire for a while to keep warm.

Her fellow lodger, Frederick Stevens, came into the kitchen at 12.10 a.m. and saw Annie, 'rather the worse for drink'. He stayed to have a pint of beer with her.

Shortly afterwards, a printer called William Stevens entered the kitchen and started a conversation with her. Annie told him she had walked across the bridge to Vauxhall in order to see her family, and that her sister had given her fivepence.

From her pocket, he saw her take a box of pills given to her by the dispensary at the casual ward of Whitechapel Workhouse. As she did so, the box broke. She picked up the pills from the floor, seized a piece of torn envelope from the mantelpiece, wrapped them inside, and left the kitchen.

William Stevens thought she had gone to bed. However, Frederick Stevens said she left the lodging-house somewhere around 1 a.m.

49

By 1.35 a.m. Annie was back in the kitchen, drunk. After eating a baked potato, she went upstairs to see Donovan in his office. He immediately asked for her doss money.

'I haven't got it', she replied. 'I am weak and ill, and have been in the infirmary'.

Donovan was unimpressed: 'You can find money for your beer and you can't find money for your bed'.

He shooed Annie out of his office.

'I'll soon be back', she said with a shrug.

Annie told him she was going up the street to find the 'pensioner', Ted Stanley.

Nightwatchman John Evans, who was asked to escort her off the premises at about 1.45 a.m., stared after her as she tottered off along Paternoster Row in the direction of Spitalfields Market.

'I won't be long, Brummy', she called back to him. 'See that Tim keeps the bed for me'. She was thinking of her regular bed, No. 29.

Shortly after 5.30 a.m. Whitechapel resident Elizabeth Long was on her way to Spitalfields Market. As she turned into the 'Stygian blackness' of Hanbury Street, she saw Annie talking to a man on the pavement only a few yards from No. 29. The premises might comfortably have housed six residents, but were occupied by seventeen, including a Mrs Harriet Hardyman and her sixteen-year-old son who cut up and sold cat meat; Mrs Amelia Richardson who manufactured packing cases; Mr Walker who made tennis boots; and two unmarried sisters who worked in a cigar factory. Like most properties in Hanbury Street, it was full of broken windows.

The man Annie was carrying on with seemed to be a foreigner, 'Jewish-looking', a little more than five-foot tall, over forty years old, with a dark complexion. His brown deerstalker hat and dark overcoat gave him a 'shabby-genteel' appearance.

Elizabeth Long heard the man say: "Will you?"

'Yes', replied Annie.

But the voice that Albert Cadosch heard only a short time afterwards most emphatically screamed 'No!' Cadosch later confirmed:

> I live at 27 Hanbury-street, and am a carpenter. 27 is next door to 29, Hanbury-street. On Saturday, Sept. 8, I got up about a quarter past five in the morning, and went into the

yard. It was then about twenty minutes past five, I should think. As I returned towards the back door I heard a voice say 'No' just as I was going through the door. It was not in our yard, but I should think it came from the yard of No. 29.... I went indoors, but returned to the yard about three or four minutes afterwards. While coming back I heard a sort of a fall against the fence, which divides my yard from that of 29. It seemed as if something touched the fence suddenly.

Thinking no more of it, Cadosch went off to work.

John Davis, who lodged in the front attic room on the third floor at 29 Hanbury Street, went to bed at eight o'clock on Friday 7 September. 'I was awake from three a.m. to five a.m. on Saturday', he testified, 'and then fell asleep until a quarter to six, when the clock at Spitalfields Church struck. I had a cup of tea and went downstairs to the back yard....'[20]

Reaching the end of the narrow passageway, he stood on the back step and opened the door. Lying on the ground before him, in between the steps and the fence, was the body of a woman, her petticoats turned up to reveal striped stockings. Her face was deluged with so much blood that he did not notice the wound to her throat. A piece of leather apron lay close by on the ground.

Inspector Joseph Chandler and other officers from Commercial Road Police Station hurried to the place, and before the body was removed from its position, divisional police surgeon George Bagster Phillips was called to examine it. By the

Hanbury Street, where Annie Chapman was murdered. (www.jack-the-ripper-tour.com)

Steps leading to backyard, 29 Hanbury Street, where Annie Chapman's body was found. (www. casebook.org)

time he arrived at 6.30 a.m. it was sufficiently light to see the full extent of the woman's injuries. Her throat had been cut and her stomach mutilated.

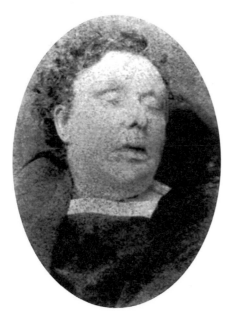

Annie Chapman's mortuary photograph. (Pinterest)

In Phillips's opinion, the perpetrator had used a very sharp knife with a thin, narrow blade, at least six to eight inches in length – the sort of knife that a slaughterman carried. The killer had grabbed her by the chin and had partially strangled her before cutting her throat and trying to sever her head.

Annie wore everything she owned, including a long black coat that came down to her knees, a black skirt, two bodices and two petticoats. Underneath her skirt and tied around her waist with strings was a large pocket, empty of contents. Her boots were laced up over red and white striped woollen stockings. Around her neck she wore a scarf, white with a wide red border, and knotted at the front.

Her body was taken to Whitechapel Workhouse Infirmary Mortuary in Old Montague Street in the same shell that had been used to transport Polly Nichols only a week or so earlier. There it was washed and laid out. According to Dr Phillips, the mortuary was little more than a shed, and 'completely inadequate to conduct post-mortem examinations'.

Whitechapel Workhouse Infirmary Mortuary, Old Montague Street. (Wikipedia, contemporary press illus.)

Later that day, Annie's brother Fountain and her friend Amelia Palmer identified her body. Annie's face had an ashen, pallid complexion, two of her lower teeth were missing, and one of her eyes was badly bruised.

The inquest, which opened on 10 September at the Working Lads' Institute, Whitechapel Road, established that her womb had been removed with a skill that suggested the killer possessed some anatomical knowledge. Her abdomen was 'entirely laid open', her intestines had been extracted from her body and placed by her shoulders. The killer had removed her uterus, upper part of her vagina and two-thirds of her bladder. Three brass rings had been torn off her fingers. The report added that Annie was already dying from an advanced disease of the lungs and brain, such as TB, or possibly syphilis.

Before these grisly findings were described, women and newsboys attending the inquest were asked to leave the room; and most newspapers ended up not publishing details of the disembowelling.

But the press did reveal the wretchedly mundane contents of her pocket: a piece of coarse muslin, one small toothcomb and another comb in a paper case, two farthings, a scrap of envelope (embossed with the words 'Sussex Regiment') two pills and some loose tea.

* * *

A wave of terror swept through the neighbourhood. Newspapers reported that mobs roamed the streets, bent on vengeance against the monster – surely not an Englishman, probably a Jew – that could commit such a dreadful crime on a woman.

At the same time, residents of No. 29 realised how they could turn the tragedy to economic advantage. Knowing only too well the human fascination in the ghoulish, they began to charge sightseers to see where Annie had been killed. Hanbury Street was soon thronging with people waiting their turn to pay a penny to enter the passageway and go into the yard where her body had been discovered; meanwhile houses opposite offered 'penny gawks' from their upstairs windows.[21] Even costermongers moved in to sell hot pies and whelks from their carts. Police tried moving people on so as to clear a thoroughfare for passing horses. But no sooner had they done so than the street filled up again.[22]

Annie Chapman's funeral took place in secret on Friday 14 September 1888. Only the undertaker, police, and Annie's relatives knew anything about the arrangements.

Shortly after seven o'clock a horse-drawn hearse, supplied by Hanbury Street undertaker Mr H. Smith, drew up outside the mortuary in Old Montague Street, Whitechapel. Her body was placed in an elm coffin bearing the words 'Annie Chapman, died Sept. 8, 1888, aged 48 years', and draped in a black pall. The casket was then taken to Harry Hawes, undertakers, in Hunt Street, Spitalfields, who were responsible for the funeral.

At nine o'clock a start was made for Manor Park Cemetery in Forest Gate. No mourning coaches followed, so as to avoid attracting public attention.

Annie's brother, Fountain, who had paid for the funeral, met the hearse at the cemetery. Her body was buried in grave No. 78, square 148. As it was a public grave, relatives were forbidden to place any headstone on it, for in due course other bodies would be buried on top of Annie's.

Only in 2008 did the cemetery authorities decide to mark the general area where Annie Chapman's remains probably lie.

Memorial plaque to Annie Chapman, Manor Park Cemetery. Located in a cordoned off area, close to the back gate. (Robert Hume)

Chapter 3

Elizabeth Stride
('Long Liz')

The Vestry Hall, Cable Street, London, 1 October 1888. Lewis Diemschütz rose and took the stand:

> I reside at No. 40 Berner-street, and am steward of the International Workmen's Club…. On Saturday I left home about half-past eleven in the morning, and returned exactly at one o'clock on Sunday morning. I noticed the time at the baker's shop at the corner of Berner-street. I had been to the market near the Crystal Palace, and had a barrow like a costermonger's, drawn by a pony, which I keep in George-yard Cable-street. I drove home to leave my goods. I drove into the yard [Dutfield's Yard], both gates being wide open. It was rather dark there. All at once my pony shied at some object on the right. I looked to see what the object was, and observed that there was something unusual, but could not tell what. It was a dark object. I put my whip handle to it, and tried to lift it up, but as I did not succeed I jumped down from my barrow and struck a match. It was rather windy, and I could only get sufficient light to see that there was some figure there. I could tell from the dress that it was the figure of a woman.
>
> [*The Daily Telegraph* 2 Oct. 1888 p.3]

That woman came to be identified as Elizabeth Stride.

On a wintry day in the last week of November 1843, a baby girl was born on a small stone-walled farm fringing the North Sea in the village of Stora Tumlehed, on Sweden's west coast. The baby's parents, Gustaf Ericsson and Beata Carlsdotter, both in their early thirties, named their daughter Elizabeth Gustafsdotter. A few days later, they took her to be baptised in Torslanda church, a quaint little building – more like a large cottage than a church.

Entrance to Dutfield's Yard, Berner Street (now Henriques Street), where Elizabeth Stride was murdered. (Jane Coram)

Elizabeth Stride's childhood home and farm in Stora Tumlehed, Torslanda, Sweden. (Photo by A. Jacobson, www.casebook.org/dissertations/elizabeths-last-stride.html)

When Elizabeth was old enough she would have been expected to pull her weight on the family farm, helping her older sister, Anna Christina, with the planting, weeding and harvesting. Her parents grew beans, peas, potatoes and cereals to sell, though sometimes barely produced enough to keep the family in food. It was tiring work, and they needed to keep their wits about them. One day Elizabeth tripped, fell and twisted her right knee.

During planting and harvest time, their parents kept both daughters off school because there was work for them to do at home. Educating girls was not thought important in those days: what did it matter if they could not write, or do their sums? There was no need for such skills on the farm; and besides, they would soon be getting married and raising a family. It was sufficient that they could read their Bibles. For her brothers, Carl-Bernhard and Svante, when they came along, it was a different matter altogether. In recognition of their higher status they were treated better than Elizabeth: they were even fed better than she was.

When she reached fifteen years old, Elizabeth returned to Torslanda church in order to be confirmed. Anna Christina did not attend the service. The year before, she had left home and moved to Gothenburg, where she had married and was now expecting a child.

Elizabeth, too, was not destined to live the quiet life on a small country farm, in a village that comprised a handful of houses. Just before her seventeenth birthday, she left Stora Tumlehed and her family in search of excitement and a new life. Following in the footsteps of her sister, on 14 October 1860 she also headed for Gothenburg, half a day's walk away, on the other bank of the River Göta älv.

The church at Torslanda, where Elizabeth was baptised and confirmed. (Wikimedia Commons)

Gothenburg in 1850. (Göteborgs Stadsmuseum)

Gothenburg was rapidly expanding into an industrial city – second only to the Swedish capital, Stockholm – and there were plans to build new houses, avenues and parks. It had a busy railway station and a daily newspaper full of advertisements for jobs. But it was also developing in a haphazard and unregulated way. With industrialization had come filth, overcrowding and poverty.

Elizabeth applied for, and on 25 October was granted, a certificate of what was called 'altered residence'. This allowed her to settle in the parish of Karl Johans, where neighbours said she was respectable, behaved well and was always reading a little Bible she carried around with her.

By February 1861 she was working as a maid for Lars-Fredrik Olofsson and his wife. Thirty-five year-old Olofsson was classed as a månadskarl, a workman who contracted out his labour to employers for a month at a time. His wife, Johanna, already had one servant but needed extra help to manage their two young boys, Carl-Otto and Johan Fredrik, and soon another child that she was carrying. The presence of the children meant that the house was full of life, and the situation offered regular employment, a roof over her head, and congenial company.

Elizabeth had been with the Olofssons for three years, and she seemed to be well settled and happy in their comfortable home. So it came as a considerable surprise to everyone when on 2 February 1864 she suddenly walked out. She did not go far, finding cheap lodgings in Pilgatan Street in the city centre, not far from the cathedral. The street was well known for its prostitutes, though Elizabeth was officially recorded in the census as a 'domestic servant', alongside scores of others.

At the end of August 1864, her life took the first of several turns for the worse when her mother died from a 'chest disease' at fifty-four years old.

Unable to find work that pleased her, Elizabeth might have returned home to care for her father. But she did not. Elizabeth was a chancer.

Instead she drifted onto the city's streets.

Without the emotional constraint of having to please her mother, Elizabeth would have felt free to break social norms, and turn down any jobs that demanded subordination and paid very poorly.

Sex work, by contrast, entailed working short hours, meant she could be her own boss, and paid relatively well. By the following March, Elizabeth, now twenty-one years old, had registered herself in the Gothenburg police files as a prostitute.

The Swedish government held a pragmatic attitude towards the sex industry.[1] Accepting that there would always be a demand for prostitutes from men incapable of controlling their sex drive, regardless of any law it might pass, it was better that the situation be 'managed'. The main concern was to keep Sweden's population strong and healthy by controlling the spread of sexually transmitted diseases, especially syphilis, which was ravaging the country.

Widely considered as a 'disease of the urban immoral', this 'self-atoned' condition began with discharges, sores and fever, and, if left untreated, eventually attacked the liver, lungs, and brain, bringing blindness, insanity and in some cases death. Many looked upon it as divine punishment for leading a wicked life.

For prostitutes, syphilis and gonorrhea, another sexually transmitted disease, were poisons that entered the body through breaches in the skin, and posed problems for their livelihood. They tried washing with alcohol and vinegar, and applied oil to their vaginal walls to prevent abrasions and infection.

In order to monitor the spread of disease and the scale of prostitution as a whole, the Gothenburg police kept two lists: List A for women who were proven to be prostitutes; and List B for women suspected of prostitution, many of whom simply happened to be walking the streets alone in the evening. Some of these latter women denied they were prostitutes, and wrote to the police in an attempt to get their name removed from the register. Enclosed with their letters were statements of good character, employment references, and the names of neighbours who could vouch that they stayed home at night.

The police made notes about each prostitute's physical appearance – their eye and hair colour, the shape of their nose, and their physical build. Elizabeth was described as being of slight stature, with blue eyes, brown hair, a straight nose and an oval face. By the side of these details was recorded the name of her church, a description of how she came to Gothenburg, if she had children, and whether she was diseased.

As a registered prostitute, Elizabeth was free from arrest, and was entitled to earn what money she could by walking the city streets, or picking up sailors around the harbour and docks. Certain restrictions were placed upon her: she was not allowed out in public before eleven o'clock at night; and twice each week she had to attend a clinic for a doctor's examination. If she showed signs of disease, she would be taken into hospital for treatment until given the all clear.

On 4 April 1865 Elizabeth was admitted to Kårhuset Hospital[2] in Gothenburg with venereal warts, and is likely to have been treated with a mixture of herbs and mercury-based pills.[3]

Kårhuset Hospital, Gothenburg. (Landala, Jan Bengston)

While in the hospital, on 21 April she gave birth to a stillborn daughter to whom she gave the last name Gustafsson.[4] The father was described in the records as 'unknown', and because the baby was illegitimate she could not be baptised.

Life had been unkind to Elizabeth. In a couple of years, between the ages of twenty and twenty-two, events had begun to spiral out of control. She was without regular work, her mother had died, and she had lost her only child.

Elizabeth was discharged from Kårhuset Hospital as healthy on 13 May.

Her time there did nothing to deter her from going back to prostitution, and at the end of August she was readmitted, this time to be treated for a venereal ulcer. After three weeks she was deemed cured, but on 17 October she was ordered by the police to return for a third visit to receive treatment for a 'venereal chancre'. When she was allowed to leave Kårhuset a fortnight later, she was required to pay regular visits to the police to prove that she was still healthy.

On a final check-up in the middle of November she was struck off the register. This was only done if a prostitute moved away, got married, or found a job. Despite the odds against a 'fallen' woman finding regular employment, Elizabeth had somehow managed to secure a job as a domestic servant. Her mistress, Maria Wijsner, wrote the police a letter accepting responsibility for her:

13 November 1865

The servant-maid Elizabeth Gustafsson was engaged in my service on the 10 of November and I am responsible for her good conduct as long as she stays in my custody.

Gothenburg, 13 November 1865

Mrs Maria Wijsner
Husargatan House No.42

And so she took Elizabeth into her home – whether as an act of kindness, or to fulfil a domestic need, is unclear, adds Dave Yost (2008). It has even been suggested that the Wijsners kept a brothel.

Two years younger than Elizabeth, Maria was the wife of Carl Wenzel Wijsner, an immigrant from Bohemia who worked for the Grand Theatre in Gothenburg. The Wijsners were Jewish, and spoke to one another in Yiddish, a mixture of Hebrew and German. The language sounded fun and Elizabeth picked up a few words.

Not long into her employment, Maria told her that she was pregnant. For Elizabeth, the news very possibly came as a painful reminder of the child she had once carried but had lost at Kårhuset Hospital. Perhaps it was because she did not want to be around when the child was born, that she gave up her situation and returned to the streets.

A few weeks later, Elizabeth was informed that her mother had left her a legacy. At last she had her own money: sixty-five Swedish crowns. To her, it was a small fortune. The direction of her life could change: she could now break free.

Within days, she applied for another certificate of altered residence – but not to some other quarter of Gothenburg, or even Sweden. Elizabeth had set her sights on moving to London, where Swedes, she was told, were treated well. She would perhaps go into service with a 'foreign gentleman', or find a situation with a family, or simply travel 'for the purpose of seeing the country'.[5] Those sixty-five crowns would give her a fresh start.

Having completed the necessary paperwork, on 2 February 1866 Elizabeth was granted permission to move to London. Five days later, she said goodbye to her family, and departed for the port. There she quickly dissolved in a great throng of men, women and wailing children, the 'huddled masses', many of whom were waiting ship for the US, to begin a new life in the land of opportunity. What would have been her fate had she joined them? Instead she had chosen a much less expensive passage to London. Elizabeth Gustafsson the domestic servant was about to become 'Elizabeth the immigrant'.

* * *

In London a young charwoman tipped Elizabeth off that servants' jobs were available in some of the grand Georgian houses that bordered Hyde Park, where the Great Exhibition had been held in 1851. The woman introduced her to a gentleman who owned one of these houses and he offered her employment in his family.

The work was not too laborious and the company was genial, but she would not receive any wages until she had worked for the gentleman for three months. Apparently this was the norm in England. Her mother's money would never last that long – probably only a few weeks.

It was then she recalled being told there was a Swedish parish in East London, where she might find friends who could help her. So, on 10 July, carrying the baptism certificate she had brought with her from Sweden, she left her position near Hyde Park, and trekked across the city to register at the Swedish Lutheran Church – a small, plain building in Prince's Square, St George-in-the-East. Elizabeth gave her address as a miserable-looking hovel she had noticed in nearby Devonshire Street, rather than reveal her recent fine abode in the West End, and was listed in the register as an 'unmarried woman'.[6]

Financed by the Swedish government and port levies, the church served the growing Scandinavian population of wealthy timber merchants, embassy staff, sailors and shopkeepers who had settled in the area in the late seventeenth century, and helped scores of Swedes and Swedish-speaking Finns feel at home in their new country. Nearby, at 33 Prince's Square, the church had a reading room where Elizabeth, if she chose, could peruse Swedish books without charge; while richer members of the congregation could buy books brought in from Sweden.

SWEDISH CHURCH, PRINCES SQUARE, E.: PREACHING THE SERMON.

Swedish Church, Prince's (Swedenborg) Square, St George-in-the-East, London, *c.*1901. (spitalfieldslife.com)

Although the existence of this little community must have been a source of comfort for her, Elizabeth soon began to realise that London was far more dangerous than she had imagined. In her very first year in the metropolis, an Irish terrorist group, known as the Fenians, detonated explosives that destroyed part of Clerkenwell Prison and several houses in the East End. Twelve passers-by, mostly women and children, were killed, and a further 120 were injured. It was to be the first of several outrages in London while Elizabeth resided there.[7]

* * *

Having given up her job in the grand house by Hyde Park, she managed to find alternative work making beds and cleaning at a lodging-house. The property, at 67 Gower Street, was situated in a comfortable middle-class area behind the British Museum, and was run by an elderly widow.

The lady gave her Saturday afternoon off, and she would spend it by going back to Hyde Park for a walk. It was there that she met carpenter John Thomas Stride. The son of a Methodist shipwright from Sheerness on the Isle of Sheppey, Kent, he too had grown up close to the North Sea, and had also lost his mother when she was in her fifties.

Elizabeth's ideal lover was perhaps tall and slim, with a moustache that curled at the corners, softly-spoken, and a man who wore well-fitting clothes. Stride was none of these things: he was short and stocky, his face resembled a potato and was stubbled, his voice loud and coarse, and he had never had the money, or inclination, to venture into a tailor's shop in all his life.

When she met him, Elizabeth had been courting a younger local man: it had taken several dates with him before he was prepared to admit he was a policeman. Stride, who lived at 21 Munster Street, Regent's Park, was forty-eight years old, almost twice her age, but he came across as an honest type, and she soon chose him over the policeman. Besides, carpentery should provide them with a steady income. She was convinced that she had met her man.

On Sunday 7 March 1869 Elizabeth Gustafsson married John Stride, not at the Swedish Lutheran Church at St George-in-the-East, but at St Giles-in-the-Fields, an Anglican church in the West End. In the latest of a series of pranks and deceptions, the bride fabricated an entry for her father in the register, recording him as Frederick Augustus, the name of John's younger brother.

A common lodging-house kitchen in the East End. (jack-the-ripper.org)

At this time, the majority of upper and middle class married women were not expected to undertake any paid work – with the exception of 'respectable' employment as a governess, music teacher or a nurse. But for working-class people like the Strides, the wife would have to work to help pay the rent and support a large family.

That summer, John and Elizabeth moved into the East End, where rents were much lower, and found a room in a lodging-house for foreign seamen in Poplar High Street. Stride's Methodist background had taught him the virtues of working hard and saving for the future, and he was excited by the prospect of running a little business. So they opened a coffee shop (or 'hall') in East India Dock Road, Poplar, close to Chrisp Street market. It was really John's brainchild. Elizabeth was not convinced: a business meant keeping accounts and checking receipts. As for the idea of accumulating money and saving it for a rainy day, to her all that probably mattered was the here and now. Today was their rainy day.

There were already more than 1,500 coffee shops in London at this time. They usually charged a penny or twopence per cup, and also sold buns and pastries. Once they had been places where customers would spend the day reading the newspaper, smoking and discussing politics.[8] However, their heyday was over, and many coffee houses had become 'greasy, dirty places [where] table-cloths and napkins are unknown. A man eats in the midst of debris left by his predecessor', and has to wade through 'the muck and mess that covered the floor'.[9]

Nobody ever thought much of the quality of the coffee. Jack London commented: 'You cannot obtain coffee in such a place for love or money…. you will have brought you something in a cup purporting to be coffee…. [but] coffee it certainly is not.' It was more like 'slops' or what he called 'water-witcheries'.

Less reputable 'coffee houses' doubled up as houses of ill fame, and advertised 'beds', not for a night's rest but by the hour. John was adamant that their coffee shop should be a wholesome and respectable establishment. But Elizabeth cared not a jot about morals and rules. What bothered her was that she and John had taken on too much work.

Seeing as the docks, goods sheds, and a railway lay close by, it seemed the ideal place to start a new business. Yet, for whatever reason, it did not go well, and in 1870 they relocated around the corner to see whether they might have more luck in Upper North Street. By the following spring, they had moved again, to open a third coffee shop at 178 Poplar High Street, even closer to the docks and the busy railway goods depot.

Elizabeth, who was known affectionately to the customers as 'Long Liz' – perhaps due to her long face, or maybe because a long step is a stride – ran the coffee shop while John continued with bits of carpentry. For a while, business was not too bad. But their future looked uncertain, and when John's father died on 6 September 1873, leaving him nothing of his hoped for inheritance, their prospects looked gloomy.

If only coffee houses were allowed to serve alcohol, Elizabeth thought. Better that they had taken on a pub. She felt sure they could have made a success of managing one like *The Blakeneys Head* opposite them. The letters of its name, curved onto a decorative iron sign above the porch, gave hordes of customers a warm welcome.

Elizabeth too would look forward to her daily tipple inside. She was a familiar face among the regulars, who called her 'Mother Gum', because when she laughed she exposed lots of missing teeth. Unlike their coffee shop, the pub did good business. They could have done well with a place like that. But her husband, a determined teetotaller like most Methodists, would never even set foot in such an establishment, let alone manage one.

Their business never picked up, and in 1874 the couple gave up the idea of a coffee shop. It would now mean scratching out a living as best they could from carpentry and domestic work.

We hear nothing of Elizabeth for three years, until 21 March 1877, when a police constable escorted her from the Thames Magistrates' Court in Stepney, to Poplar Workhouse, where she was registered as an able-bodied inmate, and made to earn her food and a roof over her head.

Poplar Workhouse dining hall, *c.* 1903. (Courtesy Peter Higginbotham/workhouses.
org.uk)

John's strong Methodist beliefs made him determined to pursue
respectable work, mainly carpentry jobs, when they came along. But
Elizabeth would not stop at anything to make ends meet when she left
the workhouse.

Life in London had turned out far differently from what she had
dreamed. Not for one moment had she imagined that she would be worse
off in what was supposed to be the wealthiest city in the world than in
the slums of Gothenburg.

So, when an opportunity to try and improve their situation came her
way, she welcomed it with open arms.

As the paddle steamer *Princess Alice* was making her return journey
from Gravesend to London Bridge on 3 September 1878, the vessel
suddenly collided with the collier SS *Bywell Castle,* and sank near North
Woolwich Pier. Within a few minutes over 650 people had died.[10]

The Lord Mayor of London organised a public collection, known
as the Mansion House Fund, to help support families who had lost a
breadwinner in the terrible disaster. Now was her real chance, and she
could not pass it by. She would pretend that her husband and a couple
of her children were among the dead, leaving her with seven other little
mites to provide for. Those who contributed to the fund could well afford
to do so, she might have reasoned. All of them were wealthy tradesmen
and shopkeepers, with plenty of spare money to travel and buy fine food.

Princess Alice disaster in the River Thames, 1878. (*Harper's Weekly* 12 Oct. 1878, Wikimedia Commons)

The incident could even be used to explain her missing upper front teeth: another passenger had kicked them out as they were climbing one of the ship's masts to escape.

All these claims were, of course, completely false. The Strides were not even aboard the ship. How could they possibly have afforded the fare? 'Mother Gum' was already known for her missing teeth. The only child Elizabeth had was stillborn in the hospital back in Gothenburg. John did not die in the disaster, as she freely acknowledged that winter when she appealed to the Swedish Church for help because of 'her husband's illness'.

Her claim was dismissed.

Always short of money, by 1881 the couple had moved into much cheaper lodgings at 69 Usher Road in Bow, which they shared with two other families – nine people in all.[11] With so little space to themselves, unable to find work, and reliant on whatever the Swedish Church gave her, Elizabeth longed for the open countryside of her childhood back home in Sweden.

Alcohol gave her some consolation. In the evenings she returned home tipsy, and began to quarrel with her husband, who would rebuke

Whitechapel Workhouse Infirmary, women's ward. (Courtesy Peter Higginbotham/ workhouses.org.uk)

her for resorting to 'the demon drink'. After one particularly bitter argument a few days before Christmas, Elizabeth walked out, and moved into a lodging-house in Brick Lane. Her health began to decline, and that winter being very cold she became ill. A few days after Christmas she was admitted to the Whitechapel Workhouse Infirmary at Baker's Row, suffering from bronchitis and exhaustion.

Following a week's recuperation, alongside other patients suffering from bronchitis, ulcerated legs, infected scalps, and general 'debility', she was considered well enough to leave the Infirmary and was sent to Whitechapel Workhouse at South Grove.

Three days later, having regained some of her strength, Elizabeth discharged herself. She was not asked to leave, and might have stayed longer, but was determined to do what she could to live by her own means – whether by doing people's laundry, scrubbing the front steps of their houses, or taking a worn collar off a shirt and reversing it.

However, she was unable to find work, and having nothing to pay the rent at Brick Lane, she moved into a common lodging-house at

Flower and Dean Street, 1902. (*Daily Mail* online 6 June 2014)

32 Flower and Dean Street, whose residents owned little more than the clothes they stood up in. Many were even without a towel, cup or saucer they could call their own.

John Stride was also facing hard times. Little carpentry work came his way; and heart problems meant him turning down any heavy jobs he was offered. In August 1882 he was forced to seek refuge in the Poplar Union Workhouse. From there, he was transferred to the adjoining Sick Asylum where, two years later, he was to die of heart disease, aged sixty-three. During the whole of that time, Elizabeth continued to maintain to the trustees of the Mansion House Fund that he had already died in the *Princess Alice* disaster.

John Stride had at least offered her a shilling or two every so often. Now that he was gone, she had nobody to turn to.

If she was lucky, on Saturdays she might find work in the homes of Jewish families, lighting fires, cleaning and sewing. London housed some 60,000 Jews, fleeing persecution in Russia and Poland. In the stretch between Commercial Road East and Little Turner Street, social investigator Charles Booth noted that practically every inhabitant was Jewish, many of them tailors. Elizabeth liked their company, and remembered a few words of Yiddish from the time she worked for the Wijsners, back in Gothenburg.

But there was no guarantee of work, even on the Sabbath, because other women often got to the jobs before her. As for other days, when there were no fires to light, and no cleaning or sewing to be had, she would go back to the only other tried and tested way she knew to earn money – by selling herself.

In London, unlike Gothenburg, she could not register with the police as a prostitute. Making sexual advances on the street was also illegal, as she found to her cost a few weeks after her husband's death on 13 November 1884, when she appeared at the Thames Magistrates' Court for being drunk and disorderly, and soliciting between Commercial Road East, and Stratford and Bow. She was not even able to sell herself without risking arrest. Elizabeth was sentenced to seven days' hard labour. This meant at the very least mending ships' ropes ('picking oakum'); and may have involved walking side by side with other women prisoners on a treadmill – a never-ending staircase with steep steps, holding onto a rail to steady herself as she was forced to keep pace with her fellows.

Artist's impression of Michael Kidney, who lived with Elizabeth Stride during her last three years. (Wikipedia)

On her release, she knew she had to seek the support of another man until things improved – one with at least semi-regular employment. Irish dock labourer and former army man, Michael Kidney, with his drooping moustache and spotted neckerchief, fitted the bill nicely. Eight years younger than her, he was still in the prime of life. They began to live together – on and off – as lovers.

Dock work being casual, the couple was never sure whether they could afford a bed for the night. When they could, they appear to have slept in a common lodging-house in Dorset Street. Situated in the 'Wicked Quarter Mile', the street was notorious for its gang murders, and no sane person would venture down it after dark. It was all such a different world to the respectable neighbourhood she had lived in with the gentleman's family when she first arrived in London.

Elizabeth Stride might easily have given up on life and turned to full-time prostitution. Instead she planned on leaving the streets as soon as she could, when times improved. She took on work cleaning lodging-houses, and making items of clothing, always carrying with her buttons, a thimble, and some wool wrapped around a piece of card.

Fellow lodgers described her as a very popular and good-natured woman. One said that she would 'do a good turn for anyone'. Others praised her for being hard-working, an able cook, and expert at the sewing machine, knitting, and all kinds of needlework.

When docking and sewing enabled them to put a few shillings together, the couple moved into a room of their own at 36 Devonshire Street. But Elizabeth missed her friends from the big lodging-house kitchen in Dorset Street, and she became restless. Her frequent absences from home, and bouts of heavy drinking, made Michael Kidney angry. Discovering her soliciting on the streets one night, he hit her, dragged her back to their room, and padlocked her in. Who knew what would happen when the next row broke out? He might beat her to death. The only thing for it was to leave him.

Dorset Street, Whitechapel, 1902. (Jack London *The People of the Abyss,* 1903, Wikimedia Commons)

Out on the capital's streets, relations between workers and employers were no less stormy. Early in 1886 labourers protesting against job losses and wage cuts had marched from Trafalgar Square to Hyde Park. Rioting followed, windows were smashed, shops looted.

* * *

Elizabeth's name continued to appear regularly in the *Fattigvårdsbok*, a book used by the clerk of the Swedish church, Sven Olsson, to note down the names of poor Swedes in the East End, and how much money he awarded them. Olsson remembers Elizabeth as 'very poor', and needing something to pay for a roof over her head, now that she was not living with her man.

With nothing left for a bed for the night, on 21 March 1886 she applied for admission to Poplar Union Workhouse, where her husband had spent some of his last days. Staff found her in such a rundown condition that they immediately transferred her to St George-in-the-East Infirmary, Princes Street.

On the streets once more, she did not know which way to turn. The Swedish Church again granted her money on 20 and 23 May 1886.

Elizabeth went back to Kidney, but their relationship went from bad to worse. On 6 April 1887 her friends persuaded her to bring allegations of assault against him. However, as in the case of many complaints filed by spouses then – and since – Elizabeth failed to turn up at court to prosecute. Who on earth would have believed the story of a common street woman, already convicted of soliciting?

But she had no choice other than to attend the Thames Magistrates' Court, eight times in all between 1887–88, for being 'drunk and incapable' or 'drunk and disorderly' at the *Queen's Head* or *The Ten Bells* in Commercial Street. On several of these court appearances she claimed her name was Annie Fitzgerald. It must have tickled her to think how easy it was to get away with it, to cock a snook at the authorities, just as she had fooled the Swedish Church over her address, and the registrar with her father's name, and had tried, albeit unsuccessfully, to claim on the Lord Mayor of London's Mansion House Fund.

Disorder of a different kind continued to erupt in Trafalgar Square where demonstrations by the unemployed had been taking place daily since the summer. Many out-of-work men and women also slept in the square and washed in the fountains. Under pressure from the press to

The Ten Bells pub, Commercial Road, Spitalfields. From 1976 to 1988, it changed its name to *The Jack the Ripper* and contained lurid wall decoration. Today's centrally placed bar would then have been set against the far wall, under the blue and white floral tiles. (Robert Hume)

'Bloody Sunday', Trafalgar Square, 13 November 1887. (Wikimedia Commons)

deal with the situation, meetings in the square were banned, and squatters removed. In a bloody clash between the police and demonstrators wielding iron bars, knives, pokers and bits of gas pipe on 13 November 1887 (London's 'Bloody Sunday'), two protestors were killed and more than 275 others were injured. Many were dockers, like Michael Kidney, demanding sixpence an hour pay – the docker's 'tanner'.

That winter, Elizabeth again went back to live with Kidney. 'She always returned without me going after her', he said later. 'I think she liked me better than any other man.'[12]

So bound up were they with their own problems, that the discovery of the body of a middle-aged woman called Martha Tabram, lying in a pool of blood not far away in George Yard, Whitechapel, on 8 August, caused little interest to them.

The old arguments soon broke out again. The fact of the matter was that Kidney could not tolerate a woman who drank. It all proved a great irony when, the following month, he was sent to prison himself for three days for using obscene language, and being drunk and disorderly.

Elizabeth had no money to pay for her lodging while he was inside, and was admitted into Poplar Union Workhouse where she was given bread, broth and a bed in return for cleaning and sewing.

Kidney's release from prison led to more quarrels. Elizabeth walked out again. Entrusting her cherished Swedish Bible to a neighbour for safekeeping, on Wednesday 26 September she left their lodging. Fortunately, she had secretly had a key cut to the padlock that Kidney had placed on their door: while he was at work, she was able to return to pick up some clothes.

Having already used up the money given to her by the Swedish Church on 15 and 20 September,[13] she had little choice but walk the streets of Whitechapel. It was there one evening she came across charwoman Catherine Lane, in the company of Elizabeth Tanner, deputy manager of a lodging-house she often frequented in Flower and Dean Street. When she explained that she had 'had words' with the man who she lived with, Tanner told her not to worry, that there would always be a bed for her at No. 32.

A few days later, social reformer Dr Thomas Barnardo came across Elizabeth in a kitchen at Flower and Dean Street, when he was visiting common lodging-houses in the East End. Barnardo had been so deeply affected by the area's appalling living conditions that he had abandoned lifelong plans to become a missionary in China in favour of helping the East End's destitute children. His aim was to see that every child, whatever their background, had the best possible start in life. This involved encouraging prostitutes to place their children under his care in a special refuge, where they would be educated to earn an honest living. Boys could learn carpentry, metal work and shoemaking; and girls trained to become good servants, or children's nurses.[14]

What would Elizabeth have made of him? More likely than not, she would have taken an instant dislike to the man. She did not see what business it was of his to take away a mother's child. Surely, women had every right to keep their children unless they were cruel or neglectful. It wasn't her fault that she had fallen upon hard times. Elizabeth told him that she once had two children, but had lost them both, along with her husband, in the *Princess Alice* disaster back in 1878. She made no reference to the seven children she claimed

were still alive back then. It was a variation on the same old tale she had spun to dozens of other people, the gist of which was now so vivid in her mind that even she had begun to think it was true.

Although Elizabeth gave him short shrift, philanthropists like Barnardo sympathised with the poor, making no distinction between the 'deserving' and 'undeserving', and were optimistic that they could, with help, improve their situation.

But they were the exception rather than the rule. Most wealthy people believed that the poor had only themselves to blame for their condition, and that they chose to live in filth. Being too stupid, or too lazy, the 'great unwashed' would have to endure for the rest of their lives the squalor and depravity

Thomas Barnardo (1845–1905), doctor, Protestant evangelist, and social reformer. The Irishman has been considered a possible suspect for the Whitechapel Murderer due to his medical expertise, and 'lonely childhood'; but his age and appearance do not match any of the descriptions of the killer (Barnardos).

they had brought upon themselves. This attitude helped to explain why in parts of the East End the practice of doling out food and clothes to the poor had been abolished, forcing the destitute into workhouses.

Two more women had now been murdered in Whitechapel, and Barnardo found the women and girls in the kitchen discussing the killings. They were 'thoroughly frightened', he reported. 'No one cares what becomes of us!' one woman cried bitterly. 'Perhaps some of *us* will be killed next!'[15]

However, it had been three weeks since the last murder, and many Londoners had begun to relax. Perhaps the killer had moved on, or had done himself in during a fit of remorse.

The weather was showery and windy on 29 September, and Elizabeth spent the afternoon at No. 32 Flower and Dean Street cleaning two rooms, for which the deputy paid her sixpence. Tanner was pleased with Stride, describing her as a very quiet woman who worked hard, and sometimes stayed out late at night to do cleaning jobs for Jews. A bedmaker at the lodging-house confirmed that Elizabeth would work when there was some to be had, and that a 'better hearted, more good natured, cleaner woman never lived'.[16]

Around 6.30 p.m. Stride and Tanner made a brief visit to their local, the *Queen's Head*, on the corner of Commercial Street and Fashion Street. The lamps outside were already lit, and it was starting to get busy inside as landlord Richard Dipple poured their drinks.

When Elizabeth returned to the lodging-house half an hour later, she gave her friend Catherine Lane a piece of green velvet to look after, and asked Charles Preston, a barber, whether she could borrow a clothes brush to smarten herself up, ready for a night out. He was unable to oblige.

Fellow lodgers remember seeing her in the kitchen, until she bade them goodbye and left at about 7.30 p.m. As she passed lodging-house watchman Thomas Bates at the door on her way out, he thought she looked cheerful. Bates knew where she was going: 'When she could get no work [sewing and charring] she had to do the best she could for her living....'

Later she was seen with various clients near Berner Street and Commercial Road.

Shortly before 11 p.m. two labourers caught sight of her in the company of a short man, wearing a jacket with white dahlias pinned to the right lapel. The man was described as being of 'clerkly appearance', with a dark moustache and sandy eyelashes. The pair had just come out of the *Bricklayers' Arms* in Settles Street, and stood in the doorway, sheltering from the rain. Surprised to see the man hugging and kissing her, one of the labourers shouted: 'Watch out, that's Leather Apron getting around you!' A man wearing a leather apron was believed by some to be responsible for murdering the women in Whitechapel that autumn, and leaving a piece of apron beside his last victim.

Moments later, Elizabeth and the man were seen hurrying towards Commercial Road, and they entered Berner Street by way of Back Church Lane. As they passed the pub on the corner, they could hear music and voices coming from a local clubhouse – the International Workingmen's Educational Club for Jewish Socialists.

At 11.45 p.m. Elizabeth was seen by William Marshall 'kissing and carrying on' with a man that he too described as a clerk. The man, who appeared to be English, wore a short, black, cutaway coat and a sailor's hat. They were walking along Berner Street in the direction of Dutfield's Yard, a dark, narrow court close to the club.

He heard the man say: 'You would say anything but your prayers'.

Elizabeth just laughed.

Sometime before midnight, a thirty-five-year-old squarely built man, about five foot seven inches tall, entered Matthew Packer's greengrocer's shop in Berner Street. In his company was a middle-aged woman wearing a dark dress and jacket with a white flower pinned to it.

The man stepped forward: 'I say, old man', he asked: 'How do you sell your grapes?'

'Sixpence a pound the black 'uns, sir, and fourpence a pound the white 'uns', replied Packer.

The man turned to Elizabeth: 'Which will you have, my dear, black or white? You shall have whichever you like best'.

'Oh, then I'll have the black 'uns', she said, 'cos they look the nicest'.

'Give us half a pound of the black ones, then', ordered the man.

Packer placed the grapes in a paper bag and handed it to the man, who passed them to Elizabeth.

The shopkeeper watched in amazement as the pair crossed the road and stood in the rain for almost half an hour near the board school, facing Dutfield's Yard.

While walking his beat up Berner Street next morning at 12.30 a.m., PC William Smith saw Elizabeth standing in the gateway of Dutfield's

Yard with a man who he reckoned to be twenty-eight-years-old. He wore a dark coat and deerstalker hat, and carried a parcel wrapped in newspaper.

About five minutes later, Elizabeth was seen in Fairclough Street, standing with a stoutish man, about five foot seven inches tall, dressed in a long black coat that reached to his heels. She was saying 'No, not tonight, some other night.'

At 12.45 a.m. Israel Schwartz of 22 Helen Street, Back Church Lane, turned into Berner Street from Commercial Road, on his way home. As he reached the gateway at the entrance to Dutfield's Yard, he saw a young man with broad shoulders, walking as if he were tipsy. He described him as five foot five inches tall, about thirty years old, with a fair complexion, full face, brown hair, and a small brown moustache. The man wore a dark jacket and trousers, and a black cap with a peak.

Having spoken to the woman – who answered the description of Elizabeth Stride – the man suddenly attacked her and threw her down on the footway. She screamed three times for help, but not loudly enough to alert members inside the club, nor PC William Smith who was on patrol nearby. Before running off, the man yelled out 'Lipski', the name of a convicted murderer.

At about 1 a.m. Lewis Diemschütz, a carter, who was employed as steward at the club, was returning from a day hawking cheap costume jewellery, trinkets and bobbles, at Westerhill Market, Crystal Palace. As he manoeuvred his pony and cart through the narrow gateway into Dutfield's Yard, so as to dump his goods before bedding down the pony in nearby Cable Street, the animal shied to the left and refused to go on.

Diemschutz suspected that something was in the way, perhaps a heap of dust or a mound of mud, but could not see since the yard was pitch-black. Striking a match, he probed forward with his whip.

Suddenly he came across a bundle on the ground. He tried to lift it with his whip but could not. Diemschutz jumped down, and struck another match. Directly in front of him was the body of a woman lying close to the club wall. Whether she was drunk, or dead, it was difficult for him to tell.

Worried about his wife, who helped him manage the club, and who was inside, he hurried into the building. It was cram packed that night because the speaker was writer and artist William Morris, leader of the Arts and Crafts movement.

Having checked that she was safe, he found a candle, and returned to the yard with two other men from the club.

Jewish Communist Louis Diemschutz was a witness at the scene of Elizabeth Stride's murder.

Scene of Elizabeth Stride's murder, Dutfield's Yard, Berner Street. (www.jack-the-ripper-tour.com)

Diemschutz struck a third match.

Looking down at the body, they could see that the woman's throat had been gashed. Mud was matted in her hair. In her left hand she clutched a packet of cachous. A little like Parma violets, smokers used these pills to sweeten their breath. They would also disguise the smell of gin. Quite possibly they were a present from Elizabeth's killer.

Next day, the newspapers reported the latest outrage by the Whitechapel Murderer. When news reached the Swedish Church that a member of their own congregation had been killed, Pastor Johannes Palmer asked Sven Olsson to go down to the mortuary at St George-in-the-East to view the body and give information to the police.

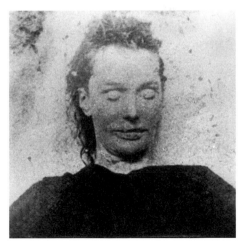

Olsson studied the woman in front of him – a slender, pale, figure with light grey eyes and dark curly hair. Elizabeth was wearing her long black cloth jacket, trimmed with fur around the bottom, the one he had always seen her in, and her usual black skirt, bonnet and checked neck scarf, knotted on the left side. 'The poor woman had had a very sad end', he reflected.

Mortuary photograph of Elizabeth Stride. (Wikimedia Commons)

Chief Inspector Walter Dew stated how 'traces of prettiness remained in her face'.

Elizabeth Stride's death certificate records that she died because of 'Violent Haemorrhage from Severance of blood vessels in the neck by a sharp instrument.' Unlike earlier victims of the Whitechapel Murderer, the rest of her body had not been mutilated, which suggested that the killer had been interrupted during his work by the arrival of Diemschütz.

An examination of the contents of her stomach found that she had eaten cheese, potato and flour before she died, and Dr Phillips confirmed that stains on her handkerchief were made by grape juice.

The grave of Elizabeth Stride (27.11.1843–30.09.1888), East London Cemetery, Plaistow. Plot 45. (Robert Hume)

Next day, Michael Kidney turned up, drunk, at Leman Street Police Station, and announced that had he been the policeman on whose beat Stride's body had been found, he would have killed himself. He boasted that he could catch the killer in the act, provided that a 'young detective' was put at his disposal.[17]

On 6 October 1888 Elizabeth Stride was buried at the parish's expense in a pauper's grave (No.15509) at East London Cemetery in Plaistow – almost a thousand miles away from the windswept farm on the west coast of Sweden where she had been born. Her funeral was sparsely attended, for she had ended her life with few friends.

Chapter 4

Catherine Eddowes
('Kate')

Less than an hour later, and only a few streets away from where Elizabeth Stride had been found, another woman was attacked.

Catherine, or Kate, Eddowes had been born on 14 April 1842 in the Graisley Green area of Wolverhampton in the industrial West Midlands, which was then part of Staffordshire.[1] When Princess Victoria had visited the town in 1830 she described it as 'large and dirty'. Few observers would have disagreed: the areas inhabited by workers and their families were squalid, and two-thirds of the houses had no sewers or drains. Cholera claimed the lives of almost 200 inhabitants, rich and poor, in 1832; and over 500 in 1848, when a report stated that one in six children died in their first year, and that life expectancy at birth was only a little over nineteen years.

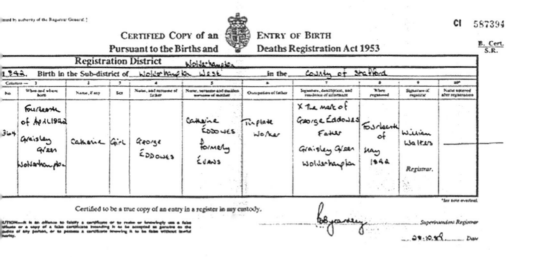

Catherine Eddowes's birth certificate. (kateeddowes.wordpress.com)

The Peacock Inn, Wolverhampton, where Catherine's mother worked as a cook. (with permission of Wolverhampton Archives)

Kate's mother, Catherine, worked as a cook at the *Peacock* on Snow Hill, a seventeenth century inn with quaint overhanging jetties, and where coaches could be boarded for Shrewsbury, Birmingham and London.

Her father, George, was employed as a tinplate varnisher at the Old Hall Works on the site of the present Central Library. For years, the company had been threatening to introduce new stamping machines and cut the tinplate workers' wages. In the summer of 1848, when harvest failure and soaring food prices spread revolution across Europe[2], the tinplate workers called the latest of a series of strikes, and Kate's father and his brother, William, who was also employed at the Old Hall Works, downed tools and went out 'on tramp', walking their families to London in an attempt to find work – a distance of over 130 miles.

Unable to obtain any, Uncle William took his family back to Wolverhampton again, where he resumed his old job. Kate's father was more fortunate, and found employment as a tinplate worker at Perkins and Sharpus. The company manufactured coppers, pots and kettles at its foundry in Bell Court, Cannon Street, in the City of London.

George Eddowes settled his wife and eight children – Alfred, Thomas, and baby George; Harriet, Emma, Eliza, Elizabeth, and Kate – first at

4 Baden Place, Crosby Row, then at 35 West Street in Bermondsey, where more of Kate's siblings were born: John, who in 1849 died from cyanosis[3], aged two months; Sarah Ann; and Mary Ann. The seven Eddowes girls, two of which, Harriet and Emma, had already left home to go into domestic service, were known as the 'seven sisters'. A twelfth child, William, born in 1854, died from convulsions, aged only four months.

Kate was a lively little thing, with a pretty face and curls, according to her big sister, Emma. Now six years old, she began at St John's Charity School in Potters Fields, Tooley Street. From there she was sent to Dowgate Charity School in Swan Lane near Cannon Street, which had been built 'for the instruction, clothing and maintenance' of poor girls. She and her fellow pupils were not expected to have aspirations to better themselves but were to be educated humbly so as to accept their position in life gratefully. What they learnt was, above all, to be useful, 'with a view to fitting them for service', and to avoid a life of vice and crime.[4] Kate was taught to read the Bible, a little writing, sewing and needlework; it was a more limited curriculum than for the boys who needed to learn arithmetic, and how to cast tradesmen's accounts. She earned herself the affectionate nickname 'Chick' because she was so little. Years later, she was still remembered as a popular classmate with a lovely singing voice.

Towards the end of 1855, when thirteen-year-old Kate and her family were lodging in Winter's Square, her mother died. Only forty-two years old, she had been suffering from pulmonary tuberculosis, an infectious airborne disease that attacks the lungs. TB, or consumption, as the Victorians called it, with its persistent cough, fever, and chest pains, was a major cause of death among the poor of London, and spread rapidly in overcrowded and filthy living conditions. The Brompton Hospital in Chelsea provided West Enders with treatment for chest complaints. However, for those living in the East End, the London Chest Hospital in Bethnal Green only opened its doors when Mrs Eddowes's situation was already hopeless.

Two years later, Kate's father also died, aged forty-nine. The Eddowes children were now orphans, and the authorities were compelled to take action. The younger ones – Thomas, George, Sarah Ann, Mary and William – were admitted to Bermondsey Workhouse in Russell Street, Southwark, on 9 December.[5] All of them were under sixteen years old, and could be detained in the workhouse if the Guardians felt they would suffer any 'injurious consequence' by leaving. And so they came to be housed alongside other orphans, abandoned children, and those born to felons and 'idiots'. Many believed that workhouses were the wrong places for children of any description, and social reformer Dr Thomas Barnardo recommended setting up proper children's homes.[6]

Shortly afterwards, on Boxing Day, three of her siblings: Thomas, George and Mary, were taken to the new South Metropolitan Industrial School in Sutton, fourteen miles south of London. Situated on a hill along the Brighton Road, the large building, recently damaged by fire, could accommodate up to 890 children. On arrival, they had to sing the national anthem to the accompaniment of a harmonium, before being rewarded with a bun and an orange.

Sarah Ann followed her brothers and sister into the school on 8 January 1858. Brother was split from sister, and made to live and work in separate quadrangles of the building; they even had to run around in a separate playground.

Contemporaries believed that much 'moral, physical, and economical advantage' could be obtained by bringing children to an out-of-town locality and placing them under a 'special discipline', instead of rearing them within the 'confined walls' of an ordinary workhouse. All were to learn a trade that would provide them with an income; and Thomas and George were also expected to carry out some digging ('spade labour') in order to 'invigorate their constitutions', and to help grow food for the school.[7]

South Metropolitan Industrial School, Sutton, 1854. (Courtesy workhouses.org.uk)

The children's only piece of good fortune was to be away from London, which was about to grind to a complete standstill. For centuries, the River Thames had been a dumping ground for human, animal and industrial waste. The summer of 1858 saw an oppressive heatwave, as a result of which all this waste began to ferment in the scorching sun. Various ways were tried to deal with the stench: MPs doused the curtains of the House of Commons with a mixture of chloride and lime, but it did little good.

Harriet, Emma and Eliza may well have smelt the pungent vapour rising off the river from their lodgings in north London, where they continued to look after their eldest brother, Alfred, who was an epileptic. By convincing the authorities they could care for him at home, they at least managed to spare him the workhouse sick ward.

Now their concern was for Kate who had nowhere to stay and no work. Seizing the initiative, Harriet wrote to their Aunt Elizabeth back in Wolverhampton to see whether she would be willing to take her younger sister in. Her aunt replied at once to say that she would welcome Kate with open arms, and would do her best to find her a situation. Harriet's mistress in Kentish Town, where she worked as a domestic servant, kindly paid Kate's fare back to Staffordshire.

Escaping from what has become known in history as 'The Year of the Great Stink',[8] sixteen-year-old Kate Eddowes left London and returned to her native Wolverhampton. She quickly came to love her new home in Bilston Street: its mysterious grand houses with tall chimneys, and walls far too high for her to see over; its little shops and pubs, interspersed with workshops where men made machine belts.

Elizabeth Eddowes treated her as if she was one of her own, and the locals took to her at once, always addressing her by name. Kate's warm smile, thick auburn hair, and sing-song voice made her the talk of the town. A further point in her favour: she apparently did not feel sorry for herself, as some orphans were prone to.

In 1861, Kate, her Aunt Elizabeth and her Uncle William were living with their three children: Lisa (9), George (4) and Harriet (1) at No. 50 Bilston Street.[9] Kate had blossomed into an eighteen-year-old beauty, whose good looks and self-confidence inspired jealousy among other young women.

The census enumerator that year had written down Kate's job as a 'scourer' at the Old Hall Works, where her uncle was still employed as a tinplate worker. Dozens of other women from the area also worked there, earning three or four shillings a week. The company specialised in the process of 'japanning', which involved decorating furniture in a fashionable, oriental style by using black varnish. Japanned ware was to be seen in almost every middle-class home.

Each morning a bell summoned Kate and her workmates along a broad pathway that led across a spacious lawn to the entrance porch. An apprentice, working when Kate was employed there, described the works as having 'the appearance of a decayed Elizabethan mansion, with large, square mullioned windows'[10], surrounded by a high wall and iron gates.

Inside the works, a grand oak staircase that had once taken guests up to the state ballroom, now led into warehouses; and what used to be bedrooms had become storerooms. In the kitchen on the ground floor an open fireplace was no longer used to roast meat for ladies and gentlemen attending feasts at the Hall, but contained vats of molten metal and grease. Kate's job was to mop up and scrub away any grease that had accidentally spilt on the floor.

Kate had only been there a short while when she was accused of stealing, and given the sack.

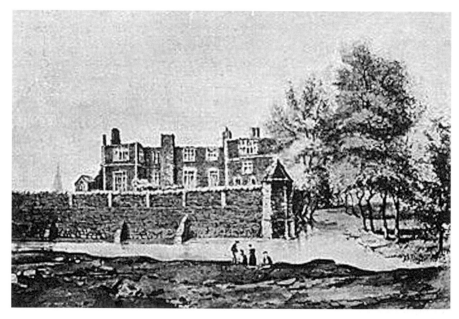

The Old Hall Works and Moat, Wolverhampton, site of the japanning factory. (*Wolverhampton Journal* 1907, reproduced on www.historywebsite.co.uk)

Aunt Elizabeth and Uncle William were furious, and told her to pack her bags at once.

In disgrace, she left for Birmingham, some twenty miles away, across the county border into Warwickshire. There she sought refuge with another uncle, Thomas Eddowes, who made boots and shoes for a living. Seeing as it was one of the biggest cities in England, she would hopefully be able to find a job there, but there was no counting on it.

Eventually, she obtained a situation as a tray polisher for a man in Legge Street: the 1861 Census records her living at House 5 in Court 12. But she worked alone and found it difficult to settle to her job.

A few months later she left Birmingham and returned to Wolverhampton, where her grandfather took her in and found her work as a tinplate stamper. While the men placed sheets of metal into a stamping press to stretch and shape it, Kate's job was to emboss a decorative pattern onto each item.

Finding the job excruciatingly dull, she quit within a few weeks, and went back to Birmingham. She craved for something that she could not put her finger on – something exciting. If she had been a young man, Kate would have run away to sea.

It was during this second spell in Birmingham that she hitched up with Thomas Conway. She had first met him in Wolverhampton when she was sixteen. Conway, or Quinn as he was known, came from Kilgeever, Louisburgh, County Mayo in Ireland, and was now in his thirties. When he was a soldier in the 18th (Royal Irish) Regiment, serving in Bombay and Madras, he had become seriously ill and was 'pensioned off'.

Those who knew Kate had doubts about her new friend. Irishness in those days was associated, at the very least, with a somewhat laid-back disposition, and, at worst, downright laziness. Being unemployed *and* Irish was a deadly combination indeed in a society that valued a strong work ethic.

Blessed by good looks and a bubbly personality, Kate could have had any man she wished but was drawn towards this young man who was never short of a yarn or two. Before long she even had his initials, 'TC', tattooed on her forearm in blue ink, and went around the country with him, telling people they were married.

At last Kate had found what she had been searching for – a life on the road, seeing new places every day. The couple travelled from place to place in the Midlands and East Anglia, peddling Conway's chapbooks. Each of these pamphlets comprised a single sheet of coarse paper, folded to make a book of between eight and twenty-four pages. Some discussed political and religious topics; others contained biographies of famous people, nursery rhymes, legends or prophecies. Each was illustrated with a woodcut, which often had little or nothing to do with the subject matter. Conway had written all of them during his so-called 'retirement', unashamedly copying much of the content from broadsheets or newspapers.

The couple came to specialise in hawking gallows ballads, for a murder could always be relied on to sell well. These grisly tales, sold at a few pennies each, described the killer's life before being convicted, gave lurid details of their crime, and what they claimed was their last confession. Each ballad had to be composed and printed within fourteen days, which was the maximum period between a criminal being found guilty and the day of their execution. In practice, Thomas managed to knock most of them out practically overnight, *en route* to Shrewsbury, Worcester and Stafford – wherever there was due to be a hanging – for every town had its printer of broadsheets and chapbooks.

Kate and Conway soon extended their patch into East Anglia, where Thomas would combine selling chapbooks and gallows ballads with any odd labouring jobs he could find.

Sometimes a gaol would turn them away, or they would fail to sell a single copy. With nothing in their pockets to buy food and a bed for the night, they would then appeal to the master of the nearest workhouse to take them in.

While she was an inmate at Great Yarmouth Workhouse, Norfolk, on 18 April 1863, Kate gave birth to a daughter, who the couple named Catherine Ann.[11] The father was recorded as a 'general labourer'. Another daughter, Annie, was also born while they were on the road in 1865.

Having left their two babies with friends, on 9 January 1866 Thomas and Kate travelled to Stafford Gaol, where some 4,000 spectators had gathered to watch the execution of Christopher Charles Robinson, which would be presided over by the infamous hangman, 'Throttler' George Smith of Dudley.

On this occasion, they were more than simply bystanders to the event: Eighteen-year-old Robinson from Wolverhampton was Kate's own cousin, who had been found guilty of murdering his fiancée.

The Reception Ward, Stafford Gaol, 1869–71. (www.search.staffspasttrack.org.uk)

Robinson's childhood had been very difficult. His mother had died when he was six years old, and a guardian had brought him up. One of his guardian's relatives, a nineteen-year-old girl called Harriet Seager, lived with them, and they began courting. Alone one afternoon, they had started to quarrel. Suddenly, neighbours heard a gun go off. Rushing round to the house, they found Robinson drunk and brandishing a razor. In the brewhouse lay Harriet, her throat cut.

At court it transpired that when she rebuffed his kisses, Robinson had become jealous that she had another admirer, punched her in the face, shot at her, and finally slit her throat. It was all recorded in the newspapers, what he had done, his trial – everything.[12] Conway had read the story out to her. Her cousin had tried to claim insanity, saying madness ran in his family; but it was to no avail.

Many years had passed since Kate had last seen her cousin but she recalled noticing a change in him. The gentle child had become sullen and withdrawn, a lazy apprentice who had taken to the bottle. But to think he had murdered the woman he professed to love and planned to marry. It beggared belief. Kate was horrified.

Conway managed to churn out an appropriate ballad in a matter of hours. Many of the verses were those he had used before. After all, Robinson was hardly the first husband to murder his wife. It was simply a matter of inserting the names Christopher Robinson and Harriet Seager in the right places.

One colourful source claims that the proceeds from sales of the gallows ballad had been so good that the couple was able to return from Stafford in style, occupying expensive inside seats on Ward's coach.

A COPY OF VERSES

ON THE

Awful EXECUTION

OF

CHARLES CHRISTOPHER ROBINSON,

For the Murder of his Sweetheart, Harriet Segar, *1866*
of Ablow Street, Wolverhampton, August 26th.

Come all you feeling Christians,
  Give ear unto my tale,
It's for a cruel murder
  I was hung at Stafford Gaol.
The horrid crime that I have done
  Is shocking for to hear,
I murdered one I once did love,
  Harriet Segar dear.

Charles Robinson it is my name,
  With sorrow was oppressed,
The very thought of what I've done
  Deprived me of my rest:
Within the walls of Stafford Gaol,
  In bitter grief did cry,
And every moment seemed to say
  "Poor soul prepare to die!"

I well deserve my wretched fate,
  No one can pity me,
To think that I in my cold blood,
  Could take her life away,
She no harm to me had done,
  How could I, serve her so?
No one my feelings now can tell,
  My heart was full of woe.

O while within my dungeon dark,
  Sad thoughts came on apace,
The cruel deed that I had done
  Appeared before my face,
While lying in my prison cell
  Those horrid visions rise,
The gentle form of her I killed
  Appeared before my eyes.

O Satan, Thou Demon strong,
  Why didst thou on me bind?
O why did I allow thy chains
  To enwrap my feeble mind?
Before my eyes she did appear
  All others to excell,
And it was through jealousy,
  I poor Harriet Segar killed.

May my end a warning be
  Unto all mankind,
Think on my unhappy fate
  And bear me in your mind.
Whether you be rich or poor
  Your friends and sweethearts love,
And God will crown your fleeting days,
  With blessings from above.

Gallows ballad composed by Thomas Conway for Kate's cousin, Charles Christopher Robinson, who was executed in Stafford Gaol, 9 January 1866. (www.casebook.org)

After leaving the vehicle at Wolverhampton, where Robinson had attacked and killed Harriet, the story goes that they hired a donkey cart and set off for Bilston. There Conway is supposed to have ordered another 400 copies of the gallows ballad from Sam Sellman, the Church Street printer, and bought Kate a flowered hat from Woolley's in Bilston High Street.[13]

We know nothing of the whereabouts of Kate, Thomas, and their two daughters for the next couple of years – and they may have returned to Birmingham.

In 1868 Kate gave birth to a son, named Thomas, while lodging in Westminster.[14]

That same year, public executions were abolished, and hanging days were no longer holidays. Their livelihood crashed overnight. Conway and Kate would have to find another way of making ends meet.

They crossed the Thames to rent cheaper lodgings on the Surrey side. The 1871 Census records them living at 1 Queen Street in Southwark. By then, Kate was calling herself Catherine Conway, and was described as a laundress, which, assuming it were true, would have involved taking in other people's sheets and clothes to scrub, dry and iron. Her partner, now aged thirty six, described himself as a peddler. Their daughter, Catherine, was now aged seven, and Thomas was three; their middle sibling, Annie, although still alive, was not recorded.[15]

Lack of regular work always kept them close to the workhouse door, and it was while Kate was an inmate at St George's Workhouse, Southwark, on 15 August 1873, that another baby, Alfred George, was born.[16] He was to be Kate's last child. Eleven days later, she and her son were discharged from the workhouse and returned to lodgings in Kent Street.

Although short of money to feed and clothe three young children, the couple tended to drink away what little they did have, and they faced heavy criticism from Kate's family for this. Conway could not hold his liquor well, and would sometimes become violent and beat her. Kate would walk out, and not return until next morning. Her sister, Emma, noticed her 'blackened eyes' when she met Kate at Christmas 1877.[17]

After one huge row while they were lodging in Chelsea, the couple decided to live apart. The children were split up: Kate took Catherine and Annie, and Thomas their two sons. Conway blamed the breakup on her drinking and frequent absences from home; but Kate's sister, Eliza, put it down to his own drinking and violent rages.

Out on the London streets – where a pub could be found on every corner, and several between the corners[18] – Kate, too, began to drink more heavily. On 21 September 1881 she was brought before the Thames Magistrates' Court, charged with being drunk and disorderly, and using obscene language.

If only she was still in Bilston Street, where she had found people so friendly. She tried pleading with Aunt Elizabeth to take her back; but she refused. She had given Kate every advantage, spared her the workhouse, sent her to school, and found her a job; yet she had repaid her by running off with Conway, who had dragged her into the gutter. What a disappointment: enough to break her poor aunt's heart.

Kate drifted towards London's East End, where she was told there was more chance of finding employment and affordable lodging. If she had a place to work from, and a sewing machine, she might have made trousers for a pound a week, even if it meant half killing herself as she bent over the long rows of stitches. But with nothing, all she could get was a few hours' work with Jewish families in Brick Lane, sweeping and scrubbing the floors of their houses, and washing their windows; or the odd bit of cleaning at the lying-in house.

Times were slack and work was not always to be found in this 'raging sea of misery', as Salvation Army founder William Booth described the area. Kate would look for cards in shop windows saying that hands were needed, but she couldn't find any. Sometimes she had nothing to pay for her food and lodging, or to buy a drink. She grew hopeless, more and more desperate. It was on these occasions when she was reduced to selling sex – as perhaps did one in twelve other poor women from time to time in the East End. They saw it as their only means of survival.

Kate had heard about the dangers. Three women, possibly more, had now been brutally killed in Whitechapel, and with the murderer still on the run some of her friends were too afraid to go out on the street. Assaults and knife wounds were an every day event, and even the police hesitated to enter thoroughfares such as Wentworth Street and Dorset Street alone.[19]

But what were her chances of coming face to face with the killer? Surely: almost nil.

'Pulling a trick', as it was known, was easy money: lifting her skirt and allowing a man a quick touch, giving a 'threepenny upright' down an alleyway. It was only two minutes' work, after all, and it paid for a drink. What choice did she have? Either that, or starve. And there were always plenty of clients: from businessmen whose prudish wives failed to satisfy their sexual appetites, to lowly clerks and labourers who had just been paid their wages and were seeking a thrill.

Now nearing forty years old, time had not been kind to Kate. She had once passed as a beauty. Men used to turn to look at her, describe her as a 'corker'. But her pretty face and curls had long since disappeared. She had let herself go, and now looked a bit rough, or 'shabby'. Often she got queasy – she put it down to a bad kidney – and she would have to stop to get her breath back in the street, right in the middle of her beat. If only she could find someone to help her and listen to her problems.

One day, near Spitalfields Market, she got chatting to an Irish porter called John Kelly. His wife had recently died, and he was seeking the companionship of another woman.

Kate started to grow fond of this gentle man who would always be buying her little somethings – a twist of tea, or a bit of ribbon – whenever he happened to have a day's work. Unlike Conway, Kelly did

Crispin Street, looking towards Spitalfields Market. (now-here-this.timeout.com).

95

not chatter away nineteen to the dozen. Her new man was as quiet as a church mouse, and was happy to sit with her and take notice of what she had to say. Another big difference to Conway was drink. Kelly said he could not afford to tipple: he had to remain sober, ready to start work portering at Spitalfields at four in the morning – otherwise he risked losing a day's pay.

When the couple decided to move in together, they knew it would mean settling for the cheapest lodgings available. Few places were cheaper than Cooney's at 55 Flower and Dean Street, a rundown, sour-smelling lodging-house in a street many feared even to set foot in, where lodgers sat on doorsteps or leaned against walls, waiting until it was time to turn in for the night. If they were lucky, a bed might be had there for as little as fourpence.[20]

Kelly later explained how they paired off and entered an extremely practical relationship: 'We got throwed together a good bit here in the lodging-house, and the result was we made a regular bargain'.[21]

The other lodgers quickly warmed to Kate's lively company, and always referred to her as Mrs Kelly. But she still had a place in her heart for Thomas, and preferred to be called Kate Conway.

Although she sometimes found floors and steps to scrub, cleaning gave her backache, and she never managed to earn more than a few pennies from doing it.

Cooney's lodging-house, 55 Flower and Dean Street. (contemporary press illustration on Wikipedia)

Friends would try to help her out by giving her clothes: a white cotton chemise; a black straw bonnet trimmed with green and black velvet and a string of black beads; a pair of men's boots with mohair laces; and a wonderful dark green chintz skirt, patterned with Michaelmas daisies and golden lilies. She would wear the lot, one on top of the other in layers, so as not to risk them being stolen in the lodging-house.

Bits and bobs would also come her way, some she had been given; others she had pilfered. Her pockets would bulge with pieces of soap, combs, a ball of string,

Artist's impression of Catherine Eddowes. (casebook.org)

clay pipes, tins of tea and sugar, a red leather cigarette case. John did not like it: to his way of thinking, being dependent on gifts from other people made them charity cases.

But whatever their circumstances and their health, at least they still had each other, and some kind of life. In March 1885 Kate received a letter from Hemel Hempstead Workhouse, telling her that her younger brother, George, had died of a brain haemorrhage. He was only thirty-nine years old.

Living always on the very brink of existence, Kate was also in and out of workhouses and their infirmaries, especially during the bitter winter of 1885–6. On 14 June 1887 she was admitted to the Whitechapel Workhouse Infirmary with a blister on her foot, probably caused by an ill-fitting boot, or one with a hole in it.[22] In the admission register she gave her religion as Roman Catholic – presumably on account of her association with her two Irish companions.

When she was discharged, she spent the whole of the next year either in the common lodging-houses of Spitalfields, if she could afford it; or, when she had nothing, in the casual wards of East London workhouses.

Longer days and warmer weather lifted her spirits, and during the summer of 1888, Kate and John walked to Kent to pick hops, as they had for the last few years. The county had several thousand acres of the crop, the flowers of which were dried in oast houses before being used to flavour beer. Hop-picking in late August and September required a big army of temporary workers, and East Enders, Romany Gypsies and Travellers from as far away as Ireland, responded in their droves. Many women and children, as well as couples, made the trek from the East End. It helped put some money together to get them through the winter ahead.[23]

After a walk of more than forty miles, by way of Dartford and Rochester, they reached Maidstone, Kent's county town. Kate bought a pair of cheap boots from Arthur Pash's shop in the high street, and Kelly purchased a jacket, which was also going for a song, from Mr Edmett, the pawnbroker next door.

As Kelly had wanted to earn every penny he could from portering, they had set off late and arrived in a place called Hunton after all the other hoppers. This meant that a lot of the jobs in the hop gardens had already gone.

Their day began at dawn, pulling down branches, or bines, from the strings, and laying them on top of a great basket, before stripping off the hops, always being very careful not to drop any leaves into the basket. At around 4 p.m. a 'tally man' weighed the hops. By being quick with their fingers they might earn as much as a shilling for each bushel they gathered.

Like other East Enders, they treated hopping as a working holiday. The air of the countryside was clean, food could be cooked on an open fire, and fresh drinking water was available from a pump. Their beds cost nothing because they slept in barns.

But it was the first time they had lived together, day in, day out, and it tested their relationship to the very limit: 'We didn't get along too well', said Kelly looking back at their time hop-picking, and we 'started to hoof it home'.[24]

He was referring to fall-outs he had had with Kate over her drinking habits. In Whitechapel she had got used to downing a 'warmer' before doing her business. For her, it was 'just a little drink' – picking hops was thirsty work, after all, she would tell him. It wasn't as if she were a 'gin-soak'.

But John hated to see a woman 'stewed', and told her to stop.

Kate gave him some lip back. To her, Kelly was becoming a bore. No doubt he would have been happy in a little house with a garden, growing potatoes and cabbages. Kate Eddowes continued to want the bright life.

On 27 September they set off back to the East End, with its horsedung-choked roads, sooty air, overflowing dustbins and stinking alleyways.

They walked most of the way with another man and his common-law wife. Before they turned off, the woman gave them a twopenny pawn ticket for a flannel shirt, saying it would fit Kelly.

As for the money they had hoped to earn, they brought back precious little.

Kelly got a fourpenny bed at Cooney's – he needed rest, for he had work the next day close by. Kate was less fortunate, spending her first night back in London in the casual ward of Shoe Lane Workhouse, Holborn, sleeping on a platform with other inmates.[25]

The next evening, Kelly lodged at 32 Flower and Dean Street, while Kate spent another night in the casual ward of a workhouse, this time at Mile End. There she declared to the superintendent: 'I have come back to earn the reward offered for the apprehension of the Whitechapel Murderer. I think I know him.'

He told her to be careful that she didn't end up murdered herself; to which she replied: 'Oh, no fear of that.'[26]

After drinking her skilly and washing floors next morning, Saturday 29 September, she went to meet her husband. The couple now had two shillings and sixpence because Kelly had pawned a pair of his boots.

Around 10 a.m. they went out to buy some breakfast, which they ate in the kitchen at Cooney's, at a table littered with bottles, jugs and books. The place was well kitted out for everyone's needs: On either side of a large, blazing fire were boilers giving a ready supply of hot water, and beneath the clock on the mantlepiece had been placed pots of coffee and tea for the lodgers to use.

Most of them were reading, knitting or having a smoke. Others, who had worked all night on the streets or in the markets, were slumped over tables, trying to catch up on their sleep.

Kate and John finished their breakfast, and went about their business.

Soon after midday, when he was on his way back from Leadenhall Market, he saw Kate again in Houndsditch. She told him she was going to Bermondsey to borrow money from her daughter Annie – that's if she could find where she lived – but planned to be back in Whitechapel by 4 p.m.

That evening, while standing, drunk, on 'Prostitutes' Island', a favourite haunt of local streetwalkers, she attracted a small crowd by her amusing attempts to imitate a fire engine's bell. At 8.30 p.m. a policeman

Leadenhall Market, 1897, where Londoners bought poultry and game. (1890swriters.blogspot.co.uk)

found her in Aldgate High Street on the pavement. When he tried to stand her up she simply fell back down again.

Police Constables George Simmons and Louis Robinson took her to Bishopsgate Police Station where Kate, smelling strongly of drink, gave her name as 'Nothing'. She was locked in a cell to sober up, and within a few minutes had fallen fast asleep.[27]

At 12.15 a.m. the next morning, 30 September, Kate was awake and singing softly to herself, as she often did.

About a quarter of an hour later she called out to ask when she would be allowed to leave.

'When you are capable of taking care of yourself', replied duty officer PC George Hutt.

'I can do that now', she replied.

Before she was released at about 1 a.m. she was asked again for her name and address.

'Mary Ann Kelly, 6 Fashion Street', she said.

Although she was still very drunk, the police figured that she would simply go home because all the nearby taverns had closed for the night.

St Botolph's Church and
'Prostitutes' Island',
Aldgate High Street.
(www.casebook.org)

She asked what the time was.

'Too late for you to get any more drink', Hutt replied.

'I shall get a damn fine hiding when I get home' she told him.

'And serve you right' he answered. 'You have no right to get drunk.'

He guided her through the passage to the front door. 'This way missus', he said.[28]

As she left the police station, Hutt told her to close the outer door behind her.

'All right', replied Kate, chirpily: 'Good night, old cock.'

Those were her last recorded words. She walked off in the direction of Houndsditch, leaving the door wide open.

At 1.35 a.m. Josephe Lawende Levy and Harry Harris saw her standing with a man at the junction of Duke Street and Church Passage, a covered walkway that led into Mitre Square, where houses huddled between towering warehouses. Her hand was on the man's chest, and they were talking together quietly. A witness described the man as about five foot seven inches tall, aged about thirty, of medium build, and with a fair complexion and moustache. He had the appearance of a sailor, and wore a pepper-and-salt coloured loose jacket, grey cloth cap with a peak, and a reddish neckerchief.

Nine minutes later, PC Edward Watkins walked into Mitre Square on his beat and began tramping along beside its tall counting houses.

Suddenly, the beam from his lantern fell across the far southwest corner and illuminated a gruesome sight. Lying on her back in a pool of blood was a woman, her clothes thrown up over her waist.

It was all completely baffling. When he had passed through only a quarter of an hour before, the square had been deserted.

Watkins raced across to Kearley and Tonge's warehouse where retired policeman George Morris worked as a night watchman.

'For God's sake mate', cried Watkins, 'come to my assistance... here is another woman cut to pieces'.[29]

Grabbing his lamp, the night watchman followed Watkins to the site of the body.

He took one look, before running off along Mitre Street towards Aldgate, blowing furiously on his whistle. It appeared that the Whitechapel Murderer had struck not once but twice in one night.

The poor woman had suffered a frenzied and ferocious attack. Yet Morris had not heard a thing. It made no sense at all, for he was always

Mitre Square, where Catherine Eddowes's body was discovered. (www.nydailynews. com, jack-the-ripper-tour.com, and Twitter)

aware of the footsteps of the policeman as he passed along Mitre Street every quarter of an hour, all night long.

From all directions, City of London police officers quickly converged on Mitre Square. Lying close to Kate's body they spotted three boot buttons, a thimble and a mustard tin. Inside the tin were two pawn tickets: one that her hop-picking companion had given her for the man's shirt; and the other for Kelly's boots, which he had pawned on his return from Kent.

Kate was taken to the city mortuary in Golden Lane, where the keeper stripped her body.

At one time she had been a real beauty, but her dark auburn hair had faded, and lay loose and filthy. Made to appear buxom by her many layers of clothing, she was, in reality, thin and scrawny. But there were some readily recognizable features. When John Kelly was called to identify her, he could do so without hesitation because of the initials, 'TC', tattooed in blue ink on her left forearm.

A post-mortem examination revealed that Kate's throat had been deeply cut, her body mutilated. Half her uterus, together with her left kidney had been removed. Her face was damaged almost beyond identity. Carved into her cheeks were V-shaped incisions, pointing upwards towards her eyes. Kate's eyelids had been nicked through, and the tip of her nose sliced off. Her left earlobe had fallen out of her clothing when she was undressed at the mortuary.[30] The coroner noted how there were no signs she had recently had sex.

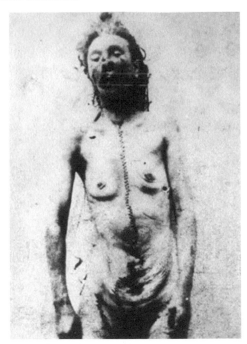

Thomas Conway took a while to hear about Kate's death, and several days passed before he turned up at the police station

Catherine Eddowes's mortuary photograph. Her body was suspended from the wall by her hair so that the photo could be taken. (Wikimedia Commons)

in Old Jewry in the company of his two boys. He told the police that he had been living in Pimlico for eight years since he and Kate broke up.

An inquest into her death opened at the coroner's court in Golden Lane on 4 October, by which time a sideshow on Whitechapel Road was displaying wax models of the murdered women.

Witnesses varied in their opinion of Kate. Her sister, Eliza Gold, who lived in Thrawl Street, Spitalfields, wept before the court, and was confused about when exactly she had last seen Kate. But she could confirm that she was a woman of 'sober habits', who used to go out hawking.

When John Kelly was called, he looked a broken man, his voice so quiet that he had to keep being told to speak up. Kelly said that he had lived with Kate for seven years, that she was good-natured. He had never known such a cheerful person: she was always singing. That when she was well enough she worked as a charwoman. How she liked a drop to drink when she had a few coppers, and it was then they sometimes had the odd tiff; though most of the time they got on well together.[31]

However, on the second day of the inquest Kate's daughter, Annie Phillips, condemned her mother as a drunkard and a scrounger. She had refused to give Kate her address in Southwark to avoid her repeated requests for money.

Still, most witnesses concurred that Kate was hardworking, generous, and jolly, and that only her fickle nature had let her down.

* * *

Hundreds of onlookers lined the streets for Kate's funeral on 8 October, and the police had to hold them back to stop anyone getting trampled on. As clocks struck one, four pallbearers carried her coffin out of the Golden Lane mortuary where a 'vast concourse of people'[32] had assembled. John Kelly, Kate's daughter Annie, and two other women walked behind her body.

The average cost of a working-class funeral at this time was over £5, which was a quarter of a workman's annual wages, and a considerably greater portion of a woman's.[33] Aware that Kate had no money, Mr G. Hawkes, the undertaker, had provided the elm coffin and funeral cortège at his own expense.

A pair of plumed horses drew the open-glass hearse, which contained Kate's coffin, resting on a swathe of purple cloth. Two carriages followed – accommodating John Kelly, and her sisters: Eliza, Emma, and Harriet.

At half past one, the hearse moved away from the mortuary. On either side of the road footpaths were lined with people, up to five deep. From the basements to the roofs of neighbouring warehouses, dozens of factory girls stood transfixed by the procession.

As the carriages wove their way through the streets, threats against 'Jack the Ripper' were voiced loudly and frequently;[34] while all the way to the Little Ilford Cemetery at Manor Park, clusters of people waited at the roadside, the men removing their hats as Kate's body passed by.

Perhaps between four and five hundred had congregated around the gates of the cemetery to witness Kate's burial in a deep, unmarked, pauper's grave. The pit would remain open until there were perhaps seventeen or eighteen coffins, interred one on top of the other.

No doubt, among the crowd were some who thought that a woman of Kate's 'type' – a 'harlot' and 'pinchprick' – got what she deserved. She was not worthy of being buried in her own grave, and marked with her own headstone.[35] They had feelings of loathing towards Kate for leading an immoral life, and would quite happily have lobbed a stone or two at her coffin. For them, the wages of sin was death.

In reality, Catherine Eddowes had been hardworking, and determined to make an independent living. It had been mainly bad luck, and the odd mistake, that had left her wretched and destitute in the streets of East London, where she met such a violent end.

Chapter 5

Mary Jane Kelly ('Ginger')

I live at 37, Dorset-street, and am employed by Mr. McCarthy. I serve in his chandler's shop, 27, Dorset-street. At a quarter to eleven a.m., on Friday morning, I was ordered by McCarthy to go to Mary Jane's room, No. 13…. I went for rent, which was in arrears. Knocking at the door, I got no answer, and I knocked again and again. Receiving no reply, I passed round the corner by the gutter spout where there is a broken window … I put my hand through the broken pane and lifted the curtain. I saw two pieces of flesh lying on the table.[1]

[Thomas Bowyer, during the inquest at Shoreditch Town Hall, 12 Nov. 1888]

The young woman – only twenty-five years of age – believed by many to be the final victim of the Whitechapel Murderer, was the most brutally killed of all. As for the earlier victims, the identity of her killer is unknown. Yet much of her life remains an even greater mystery than her death.

A girl by the name of Mary Jane Kelly was born in Limerick City, in the west of Ireland in 1863. She was baptised in Castleconnell on 31 March[2], and appears to have lived with eight or nine brothers and sisters at a house in Mungret Street, a busy thoroughfare, packed with small butchers, haberdashers, and marine stores selling ships' rope and fishermen's nets.[3]

County Limerick had been particularly badly affected by the Irish potato blight of the 1840s, when tenant farmers found themselves hungry, with no potatoes to eat, let alone sell. Unable to pay rent, many were evicted from their cottages. Nationally, over a million people died, including some 70,000 in Limerick alone, their emaciated, coffinless bodies deposited in anonymous burial pits.[4]

Mary Jane Kelly ('Ginger')

No. 13 Miller's Court, off Dorset Street, where Mary Jane Kelly lived and was murdered (*Penny Illustrated*, 17 Nov. 1888).

Those who were strong enough fled the countryside and headed towards Limerick City to seek work. Discovering there was none to be had, they began queuing outside its workhouses for a bed; while other families made for the quays, which became the departure point for hundreds of emigrant ships bound for US, Canada and Australia.

When Mary Jane was still a child, she sailed with her family across the Irish Sea to settle in South Wales, where an aunt lived in the old market town of Carmarthen. Her father, John Kelly, found employment at the iron and tinplate works situated high above the River Towy, where he was promoted to foreman, overseeing the smelting and milling.

The aunt was happy to take in Mary Jane's older sister because she had a daughter of a similar age, and thought it would be good company for her. She also obtained work for the girl every Wednesday and Saturday on a stall in Carmarthen market. From time to time, Mary Jane joined the two girls around the town, carrying big baskets of ribbon and thread, which they would attempt to sell to passers-by.

She got used to her new home, and began to learn the Welsh language, which most inhabitants of Carmarthen spoke. At first, hawking probably seemed more like fun than work. But regular jobs were scarce, and Mary Jane could not make a living from selling haberdashery. Her aunt encouraged her to find a husband who could support her. A beauty like her, with blue eyes and thick ginger hair, should have no problem capturing one.

In 1879, when she was still only sixteen, she met and quickly married John Davies, a local miner. Davies worked down a pit across the border in Glamorganshire, making a good living from excavating the much sought after 'steam coal' that was used as fuel by ships and railway locomotives.

Coalmines were dangerous places to work. Miners had to feel their way through dark and wet tunnels with the aid of candles. Ventilation was poor, and inhaling dust particles often led to long-term lung disease; while deaths due to roofs collapsing and gases such as methane exploding were all too frequent.[5]

Less than two years later, John Davies was killed in such a pit explosion.

Or so Mary Jane said.

According to one recent biographer, however, all this is fiction. Wynne Weston-Davies claims that Mary Jane Kelly was living under a pseudonym, and that she was, in reality, his great aunt, Elizabeth Weston Davies, who was already in Wales, having been born not in Limerick but in Montgomeryshire.[6]

Whatever the truth may be, there is no doubting that the woman we shall continue to call Mary Jane Kelly had been living in Wales for a number of years, when around 1880, she moved first to Swansea and from there to Cardiff, in the company of the cousin she had hawked goods with as a child.

Cardiff was fast becoming the largest town in Wales, with more people even than Merthyr or Swansea, and the two young women believed that there would be good work prospects for them there. They had heard how the city was filled with luxury shops such as watchmakers and jewellers, and that positions could be found in the fine hotels, or in a new large department store.

But they were to be disappointed. In the economic downturn that was affecting Europe and the US, jobs in Wales turned out to be scarce, and men quickly seized those few chances that came up. Before long, she and her cousin drifted into the only work that was always available for women – sex work. There was a constant demand for women who were prepared to sell themselves, just as there were always men who could not, or did not want to, settle into a relationship; or who claimed their wives 'did not understand them'.

Plenty of opportunities existed for picking up clients at the pleasure grounds, or at hotels advertising 'every accommodation for commercial gentlemen'. And if none of these gentlemen could be found, there were always dozens of sex-starved sailors at the docks looking for women, for Cardiff was one of the biggest ports in the world.

In 1880 and 1881, Mary Jane spent eight or nine months as a patient at the Cardiff Royal Infirmary, or Glamorganshire and Monmouthshire Infirmary and Dispensary, as it was known in that period[7], probably suffering from an infectious disease.

According to her friend, the artist Florence Pash, she later cleaned floors at the Infirmary on its new site in Glossop Road.[8] The glittering prospect of regular work in the shops and hotels of Cardiff had, after all, come to nothing.

Glamorganshire and Monmouthshire Infirmary and Dispensary (Cardiff Royal Infirmary), where Mary Jane Kelly stayed as a patient. (forum.casebook.org)

Mopping and polishing was no life; so, in 1884, she took the plunge and moved to London. The bright lights and the dream of meeting a wealthy gentleman drew her to Chelsea in the West End, a neighbourhood favoured by the rich as a place of residence because it was upwind of the smoke drifting from the crowded city. The district was home to grand parades of shops and luxury hotels; while along its fashionable King's Road could be found plant nurseries and perfumery gardens. Close by, in the recreation ground, there was music and dancing, an ornate fountain and coloured lamps.

Many celebrities of the day had a house in Chelsea: American-born artist James McNeill Whistler; the playwright Oscar Wilde – when he was not gallivanting in Paris or New York; and one of the Prince of Wales's many mistresses, the actress Lillie Langtry.

Artist Walter Sickert (1860–1942), named as Jack the Ripper by Patricia Cornwell. Mary Jane Kelly may have worked for Sickert's family as a nursemaid in Chelsea. (Wikimedia Commons)

Artist Walter Sickert, named by novelist Patricia Cornwell as Jack the Ripper, also had a studio in Chelsea. Sickert's family appear to have rescued Mary Jane from a casual job as a tobacconist's assistant in a shop opposite the studio, and employed her for a few months as a nursemaid.[9] She was introduced to Florence Pash, who accompanied Sickert to music halls and restaurants, and soon she became Mary Jane's friend.

When she was no longer required as a nursemaid, Mary Jane was recommended for the situation of lady's maid to Mary Cornelia Edwards, Marchioness of Londonderry. Although she owned a grand house in the Welsh market town of Machynlleth in Montgomeryshire, she was staying in London for a few months while her husband attended to some business. Mary Jane disliked her aged and reclusive employer, and when the Marchioness's husband, George, died in November 1884, she sought another situation. The prospect of returning with the Marchioness to her home in Wales, and pandering to her every need, filled her with dread.

Besides, by then a woman named Ellen (or Héleine, as she preferred to be called) Maundrell had offered her work in a 'gay house' that she ran with her sister, Frederica. Situated in Kensington, Héleine described the house as comfortable, and told Mary Jane she would be paid well.

The Maundrell sisters, who had been born in Brittany and spoke fluent French, had become extremely successful business partners. In addition to their premises in Kensington, they owned a string of 'French' middle-class brothels in St Pancras, Islington and Camden, which masqueraded as hotels or coffee houses. Although the police knew full well of their existence, they ignored them because the girls were not visible on the street to cause a nuisance to passers-by.

Mary Jane was officially employed as a lady's maid in their residence at 28 Collingham Place, a ten-minute walk away from the new Natural History Museum. The building, which boasted a portico, bay windows and balconies, comprised four main floors, a basement and dormers. It fronted as a finishing school but in practice operated as one of the classiest brothels in London, where clients paid considerable sums for the girls' favours.

Known as 'Ginger', on account of her long red hair, Mary Jane instantly became one of the most called upon girls in the house. With the considerable earnings she made, she was able to buy expensive clothes, just like a lady. She could even afford to hire a carriage and ride around Hyde Park.

A 'gay house', or brothel, at 28 Collingham Place, near Earl's Court underground station, where Mary Jane Kelly worked for the Maundrell sisters. (Robert Hume)

Wynne Weston Davies names one of her clients during these days as Francis Spurzheim Craig, a penny-a-line newspaper reporter who covered the police courts and inquests in the East End of London. Craig, who had been born in Acton, London, in 1837, still lived at home with his mother and father, a dissectionist and phrenologist who interpreted personality types by feeling the shape of people's heads.[10]

Craig had known better times. Some ten years earlier he had been editor of the *Bucks Advertiser and Aylesbury News*. He was heading for a promising career when a rival publication exposed him for cribbing reports word for word from *The Daily Telegraph*.

Now back living in his native London, he became one of Mary Jane's regulars, and in December she quickly accepted his invitation to accompany him to Paris. Craig promised there would be work for her in one of the two hundred or so gentlemen's clubs, or legalised brothels ('maisons closes' or shuttered houses), that centered on the district of Montmartre.[11]

Paris was very much the world capital of pleasure during the last quarter of the nineteenth century, the so-called *Belle Époque*. The most famous artist of the era, Henri de Toulouse-Lautrec, would stay out until the small hours of the morning, capturing in his paintings the city's fascinating nightlife – its smoke-filled cafés, theatres, cabarets and brothels, noted for their lavish sculptures, sumptuous décor, and voluptuous women. Toulouse-Lautrec spent much time in these brothels, where he was accepted by the prostitutes and madams, and lived with them for weeks at a time, painting and drawing them at work and at leisure.

Another frequent visitor to Paris's brothels was the Prince of Wales, the future King Edward VII. At Le Chabanais, which was the most luxurious brothel of all, 'Bertie' had his own richly decorated room, and his coat of arms carved above the bed. He would bathe with prostitutes in a giant copper bath filled with champagne, and is supposed to have enjoyed threesomes in a lavish chair he called his 'love seat.'

Less elaborate Parisian brothels were also easy enough to identify. Prospective clients simply had to keep their eyes on the number plates above the doors. If they were larger, more colourful and ostentatious than the standard blue and white version, they would know instantly that they had arrived at a house of pleasure.

By working for a madam, and providing sexual services for bourgeois and aristocratic clients, as well as young 'bohemian' types, Craig promised Mary Jane that she could earn enough money to set up a business of her own.

At first she found the possibility attractive. But the fabulous earnings did not materialise, and seemed never likely to. Far away from friends, and even further from her family, she became homesick within a couple of weeks, and asked Craig to take her home.

On Christmas Eve they returned to London, where he assured her that she would be able to resume the high life she had been used to, and again be able to afford a carriage. Any day, so he said, the post would bring a letter carrying news of his promotion from reporter to newspaper editor. Little did she realise how he had no more chance of reaching that position than she succeeding Queen Victoria.

With what appeared a bright future ahead of them both, she agreed to marry Craig in secret at Brook Green Register Office, Hammersmith, on Christmas Eve 1884. They had known each other for a matter of weeks, and, at forty-nine, he was old enough to be her father – but it didn't seem to matter.

The couple lived in quick succession at 3 Andover Road, Hammersmith; 7 Lemon's Terrace, Stepney Green; and 12 Argyle Square, Bloomsbury – all areas of so-called 'mixed' housing, where the poor lived close by the well-to-do, and the 'semi-criminal' class was never far away.[12]

Long before they moved to Bloomsbury, their honeymoon period was well and truly over, and both of them were beginning to reveal their true colours. Francis Craig was in reality a most odd, private man, whereas Mary Jane was vivacious, sociable and always had a smile on her face. Her husband was a miser, but Mary Jane liked to spend. Craig could not look someone straight in the eye, he seemed to be harbouring a secret, whereas Mary Jane was open, and appeared to hold no secrets from anyone. They were completely unsuited to each other, and living together soon became intolerable.

After three months Mary Jane had had enough, and one night she walked out.

The best chance for anyone on the run in London was to make towards the East End, that 'bottomless pit of teeming life', as Beatrice Webb dubbed it, where people came and went at all times of the day – and night. Containing a higher concentration of people than anywhere else in England, it was an ideal place to 'disappear' until it was safe to move back among people of her own class.

She knew that she had no hope of maintaining the life she had been used to in West London, a golden world of domestic peace and happiness; but she could scarcely have guessed that her existence would soon become a daily battle to make ends meet. In the East End life was nasty, brutish and short.

Back in Bloomsbury, Francis Craig could not cope with his loss, and decided to recruit private detectives to comb the streets in order to hunt his wife down. It did not take long for him to gather the evidence he wanted: Mary Jane had been spotted entering a private hotel at 53 Tonbridge Street, close to their very own lodgings in Argyle Square, late in the evening, in the company of a young man.[13] There was no doubt in his mind that his wife had gone back to working as a prostitute.

On 8 March 1886 his sleuths further reported that she was living at 161 Drummond Street, a well-known brothel run by Ellen Macleod, close to Euston station. There followed a number of other sightings of her with different clients in Holloway and Camden, before Craig was informed that she had taken lodgings in the East End.[14] So runs Weston Davies's version of events.

If, instead of Welsh, she really was Irish, as Mary Jane Kelly maintained, she joined thousands of other Irish immigrants who had settled in the slums of Whitechapel after the Great Famine of 1845–52. The area had even been nicknamed 'Little Dublin'. Some found casual labour in the docks and markets; many trundled wheelbarrows through the streets, selling nuts and oranges. Others, including Mary Jane Kelly, resorted to prostitution. Many thousands of women are estimated to have been walking the streets from time to time in London during the last quarter of the nineteenth century. Up to eighty per cent of their number may have been Irish, with the name 'Kelly' often being used to denote a prostitute.

The most expensive were the so-called 'gay' women, who paraded in their brightly coloured clothing outside the theatres along the Strand, Haymarket, and Covent Garden; or strolled in the Vauxhall Pleasure Gardens. Interested clients could purchase catalogues listing these women – and their specialities.[15]

By contrast, most of those prostitutes in the East End were reduced to standing on murky street corners and wandering the dark alleys between squalid tenements, plying their trade as best they could, vulnerable to attack by men who were normally civil and pleasant but having drunk away their wages had become wild beasts.

This area, with all its dangers, was the one that Mary Jane Kelly was aiming to lose herself in, for it constantly thronged with people. She could leave her past life behind: in the East End it would be difficult to track her down.

Far from Craig giving up his hunt for her, Weston Davies claims that he pursued her ever more vigorously, taking lodgings at 306 Mile End Road. By day and night he tramped the streets and alleys. His original desire to take her back had evaporated away; now he was determined to exact revenge on her. If it meant a campaign of mass murder in order to cover his tracks, Davies argues, then so be it.[16]

* * *

Mary Jane Kelly remained in the East End. Inspector Walter Dew recalled encountering her 'parading' around the district, usually in the company of two or three friends, when he was a young policeman on the beat in Whitechapel. He described her as 'buxom', with blue eyes and thick hair that reached her waist when she let it down. She took pride in her appearance, and always wore a spotlessly clean white apron.[17] People were stunned by her sudden arrival because her face did not fit at all. What on earth was such an attractive, classy-looking and educated woman doing walking in some of the filthiest, most overcrowded, and dangerous 'stews' in London – home to scores of abandoned women?

It was much more difficult to find work in the East End than Mary Jane had imagined. A person seeking regular employment in those days was expected to carry with them a 'character'. This was a testimonial of their trustworthiness and reliability, written by their former employer. Failing that, they were meant to provide the employer's name and address – preferably a local one – so that their 'seriousness of character' and honesty could be checked. But Mary Jane could scarcely give them the address of a well-known Kensington brothel.

This limited her to the meanest of jobs where no character was required. For a time, she may have worked as a domestic servant at the Nuns of Providence Row Night Refuge and Convent. The building was situated in Crispin Street, Spitalfields, and gave shelter to destitute men, women and children. But pushed to the limits by extremely long hours, meagre pay, and the drudgery of cleaning floors, she soon returned to the streets, where she could be her own boss, and choose her own hours.

The National Vigilance Association deplored the attitude of women such as Mary Jane Kelly. It believed that prostitutes who refused to repent and reform should be treated harshly. In its eyes, they were not 'women', and so did not deserve to be protected like the rest of the 'weaker sex'. By continuing to work the streets, they were public nuisances, making life intolerable for other, respectable young women who wanted to walk about in the evenings, and for young men who were unable to pass down a street without being accosted.

Mary Jane was not bothered a jot by such moral humbug, but there was still the dangerous nature of the work for her to consider. A man who wielded a knife had by then slashed to pieces at least four women in that very district. Disillusioned with the progress that the police were making to find the culprit, a neighbourhood vigilance group had been formed. But nobody was any nearer to tracking down the killer.

In St George-in-the-East, Wapping, his terrible crimes provided a constant topic of conversation for her fellow lodgers in a house along the notorious Ratcliff Highway. The long road, which ran parallel to the Thames, consisted of chandlers' shops, pubs, opium dens, and brothels that catered for seamen flushed with cash following a long voyage.

After dusk, the gaslamps and illuminated window displays gave this sordid street a kind of attraction. So-called 'sailors' women' added a touch of colour in their bright, low-cut dresses marked out with ribbons and flowers, and their painted Morocco boots with glistening brass heels. Walking in droves, and showing off their calves, they shouted excitedly to one another across the road before disappearing into bars and dance halls.

A Dutch widow, Mrs Eliesabeth Boekü, took Mary Jane into her house nearby at 79 Pennington Street. She was in business with a skinner by the name of Johannes Morganstern, and ran a brothel that was popular with sailors. Mary Jane became one of their girls.

Ratcliff Highway, St George-in-the-East, 1896. (pubshistory.com)

By all accounts, she was different to the other local prostitues, being younger and prettier; but like them she quickly started to fritter away her takings on drink, which gave her much needed courage to satisfy the demands of difficult clients.

Her drinking habit soon got her into arrears with the rent. Determined that she should pay at least some of what she owed, Boekü escorted her back across London to Knightsbridge to collect a box of expensive gowns left at the Maundrells, which she accepted as payment.

Mary Jane needed cheaper lodgings, which she found with Mrs Mary McCarthy at 1 Breezer's Hill. The street's narrow, gas-lit cobbles, overshadowed by tall, soot-stained warehouses, certainly afforded a dismal contrast to the glamorous well-lit streets she had been used to in the West End.

When she introduced herself, Mary Jane told Mrs McCarthy that she was Welsh, but on a later occasion she claimed she had been born in Limerick, and had travelled to Wales as a baby when her father was looking for work in the iron industry.[18]

McCarthy, like Mrs Boekü, kept a brothel. Although the Criminal Law Amendment Act of 1885 made this practice illegal, the police had not the resources or interest to enforce the regulation, and her house was ever popular with sailors because it was so close to the docks.

Her employer commented how Mary Jane came from a more privileged background than the other girls, was better educated, and was 'no mean artist'. When sober, she was 'one of the most decent and nicest girls you could meet'.[19]

Each time she ventured out, she wore a smart jacket and a hat. Although described by some as 'stout', she seemed plumper than she really was because she wore all the clothes she owned, one item on top of the other. Only a fool would rely on their property still being intact when they returned to their lodgings. And Mary Jane Kelly was certainly no fool.

* * *

Sometime towards the end of 1886, she suddenly left Breezer's Hill. It is understood that an older man was looking for her. That older man was perhaps Francis Craig.

For the next four or five months, her whereabouts is unknown. Maybe she stayed with Johannes's brother, Thomas Morganstern, who she had met two summers before, and who lived near the gasworks in Stepney. We do know that she lodged briefly with one of her clients, a mason-plasterer from Bethnal Green, called Joseph Flemming. According to Mrs McCarthy, Flemming wanted to marry her.

By spring 1887 Mary Jane had moved into Spitalfields, where she slept at Cooney's, a very poor lodging-house in Flower and Dean Street, close to the junction with Brick Lane. Each evening she would walk up and down Commercial Street, soliciting market workers, drinking heavily, and returning to the lodging-house in the early hours to sleep.

How she tried to prevent herself becoming pregnant we do not know. Some prostitutes used acidic powders and jellies to try to kill sperm; others employed homemade pessaries made from cocoa butter. A few who could afford it may have fitted 'womb veils' – forerunner to the modern diaphragm and cervical cap – which blocked sperm from reaching the uterus.

On Good Friday, 8 April, while she was in the *The Ten Bells* on the corner of Fournier Street, she got into conversation with a fair-haired, blue-eyed cockney. Irishman Joseph Barnett was older than she was, in his thirties. A rather awkward and nervous man, his habit of repeating the last few words of anything said to him before replying made him a figure of fun.

Some years before he had lost his licence as a porter at Billingsgate fish market, where his three brothers also worked. That licence had guaranteed him work, carrying around fish at fixed hours at a regular wage. Now he was reduced to working as a casual market labourer and fruit-porter, with no certainty about what he could make.

Kelly told him she made a living by selling flowers, that her real name was Davies, and that she had been married to a young Welsh miner who had been killed in a pit explosion. Irish by birth, she was still receiving letters from her mother back in Ireland. She was proud of having travelled to France, and said that since returning she preferred to be called 'Marie Jeanette'.

When they met again the next day, Mary Jane and Joe decided that, for economy's sake in straitened times, they might just as well live together. The couple drifted from one common lodging-house, or 'doss-house', to another, paying for their bed a few pennies per night. Their sheets were filthy because lodgers dared not remove their boots for fear of them being stolen in the night and pawned. In the morning they shared an outside privy and washbasin with fifty or more other residents.

But no matter how foul their living conditions, it was infinitely preferable to going into a workhouse. On the outside they were at least free.

From George Street they moved to Paternoster Row, to Dorset Street in Spitalfields. Once the centre of the silk industry, Dorset Street had gradually descended into 'debauchery, vice and violence', and was now the resort of thieves and murderers. Notorious, as previously stated, for being 'the worst street in London', its warren of old buildings and maze of alleyways housed an underclass that was 'avoided and ignored by much of Victorian society'.[20]

In the spring of 1888 Mary Jane and Joe began renting a ground floor room at 13 Miller's Court, a fetid cul-de-sac, located down a narrow, three-foot-wide, arched passageway off Dorset Street. 'A big man walking through it would bend his head and turn sideways to keep his shoulders from rubbing against the dirty bricks.... Misery is written all over the place, the worst kind of London misery.'[21]

Above: The archway connecting Dorset Street with Miller's Court. (Photo by Leonard Matters 1928, Wikipedia)

Below: No. 13 Miller's Court. (Wikipedia)

Numerous other prostitutes lived in the court. As there was only one entrance and exit into the yard, clients could be observed coming and going, and the women tried to offer one another mutual protection.

The place shared by Mary Jane and Joe was not even a complete room: it was the dingy, partitioned-off, ground floor back room of 26 Dorset Street. One newspaper described it as a 'miserable apology for a dwelling',[22] not more than twelve foot long and ten foot wide, uncarpeted, with an ancient wooden-framed bed, two small tables and two chairs. Clothing dangled from the windows in place of curtains, and a framed print[23] hung forlornly above the small fireplace.

Mary Jane would get Joe to read aloud from the newspaper about the Whitechapel murders. One of the victims, Annie Chapman, she had come across from time to time, drinking in *The Britannia*. The awful killings, especially the mutilations, terrified her.

Money continued to be very tight and work was hard enough even for men to find. Joe could only get casual labour in the markets; the rest of the time he sold oranges in the street.

But for a woman it was much more difficult, and Mary Jane

often had to go with men for as little as fourpence a touch. What choice did she have? It brought in much needed cash.

Her youth and good looks meant she had no shortage of pick-ups as she worked a beat in the area around Leman Street, down towards the docks, before returning to Commercial Street, closer to home. It was all very different to the protected existence she had led in brothels frequented by well-heeled gentlemen in the West End, or by Parisian aristocrats. Her clients were now beer-sodden clerks and labourers who had just been paid.

In Whitechapel, life was raw and dangerous. Robbery and muggings were an everyday event. She would have to stand up for herself. As a boy, retired market porter Dennis Barrett knew Mary Jane Kelly by sight. By now, she had started to dye her hair, and it was this and her sudden fierce temper, especially when she was drunk, that got her known as 'Dark Mary'. She had her pitch outside the *The Ten Bells* pub in Commercial Street, 'and woe to any woman who tried to poach her territory. Such a woman was likely to have her hair pulled out in fistfuls.'[24]

Joe did not like what she did to get by. So much for the yarn she had spun him about 'selling flowers' for a living. The truth was that she earned a living from selling *herself*. As far as he was concerned, she was a 'tart'.

And yet, they managed to get along – more or less – and locals remembered them as a friendly, pleasant couple, giving little trouble except, occasionally, when drunk. That was when she might get quarrelsome and cause a nuisance. On 19 September 1888, a woman called Mary Jane Kelly was fined two shillings and sixpence at the Thames Magistrates' Court for drunken disorderliness. Towards the end of October, she broke the window of 13 Miller's Court when drunk. It would prove a godsend when she and Joe lost the doorkey because they were able to reach through the broken pane, and pull back the bolt.

Now the days were drawing in, and it was getting colder. Pitying her friends who had no lodging, one night she brought a couple of women back to share their room. Joe could not stomach this, and on the evening of 30 October they argued like they had never done before when she brought back a prostitute called Julia Venturney.

* * *

The Whitechapel Murderer had been inactive for over a month, and Mary Jane, like many other prostitutes, began to feel that it was safe to return to the streets, to walk her beat. Besides, the rent had to be paid. Four shillings a week, due every Monday – 'Black Monday', as East Enders called it. They were now thirty shillings in arrears, putting her under increasing pressure to earn some money, no matter how. She did not have the luxury of staying inside at night behind locked doors that some women had.

Washerwoman Mrs Maria Harvey stayed with them on 1 November. She was another 'unfortunate' who had been thrown out by her husband. Joe did not like it. When she returned to stay with them again on 5 and 6 November, it proved too much. Whatever Mrs Harvey's circumstances, to his mind she was a woman of 'bad character'. Her presence defiled their little house. He could not accept it. That evening he walked out.

Although he still visited Mary Jane every so often, and gave her what little money he could spare, they were never to live with each other again.

Next day, Mary Jane bought a halfpenny candle at John McCarthy's chandler's shop, 27 Dorset Street, on the corner of Miller's Court. As she handed over the coin, she joked about the Whitechapel Murderer: 'That dreadful man! Ain't he a caution! I wonder who he'll have next?' But her friends said that, despite her quips, deep down she was frightened by the murders and contemplated leaving London.

Later that day, rent collector Thomas Bowyer saw her in Miller's Court talking to a smart man in his late twenties with a dark moustache and 'very peculiar eyes'.

The following afternoon she spent with Maria Harvey, and the early evening with her friend, Lizzie Albrook.

'Whatever you do, don't you do wrong and turn out as I did', Lizzie told her.

Mary Jane replied that she was heartily sick of her life on the street and wished she had enough money to go back to Ireland where her people lived.

Joe called on her that evening between 7.30 and 8 p.m. while Lizzie was there.

Her neighbour, Mrs Elizabeth Prater, chatted to her at about 9 p.m. by the arch, before they went off in different directions to look for clients. Dressed in her usual smart jacket and hat, Mary Jane appeared to Prater as 'tall and pretty, and as fair as a lily'.

'I hope it will be a fine day tomorrow', Mary Jane told her, 'as I want to go to the Lord Mayor's Show.'[25]

Elizabeth said to the younger woman: 'Good night, old dear.'

Mary Jane answered: 'Good night, my pretty.' She always called her that.

The rest of the evening she spent drinking at the *The Britannia* in Dorset Street, where she was seen, very tipsy, in the company of a young man with a moustache. Later she was sighted in the *Horn of Plenty* and *The Ten Bells*.

At about 11.45 p.m. Mrs Mary Ann Cox, who lodged in Miller's Court, saw her in a linsey frock and red knitted shawl, coming home very drunk with a stout, shabby, blotchy-faced man in his thirties. The man had a carroty moustache and a billycock hat, and was carrying a quart pail of beer.

She called out, 'Goodnight Mary.'

Mary Jane mumbled something back about going into her room to sing.

And sure enough, early in the morning of Friday 9 November, several witnesses heard her singing. She usually sang Irish songs. This evening it was the favourite music hall ballad: 'Only a violet I plucked from my mother's grave.'

At 12.30 a.m. a neighbour, Catherine Picket, considered going to complain about the singing but her husband told her to 'leave the poor woman alone'.

George Hutchinson, an unemployed labourer and groom who knew her well, came across Mary Jane at 2 a.m. on the junction of Flower and Dean Street, and Commercial Street. She asked him for sixpence but Hutchinson said he had nothing on him.

Soon afterwards, a labourerer was seen tapping her on the shoulder. The man, who was aged thirty-four or thirty-five, and five foot six inches tall, had a pale complexion, dark hair, and a moustache curled at each end. He was described as respectable looking, of Jewish appearance, and wore a long dark coat with a red kerchief. They made off together, his arm around her shoulder, and were seen passing by the *Queen's Head* pub, laughing, before they disappeared under the arch into Miller's Court.

Shortly before 4 a.m. Sarah Lewis, who was staying at 2 Miller's Court, heard someone wail 'Oh murder!' but took no notice because it was such a common cry in the East End.

In the room above Kelly, Elizabeth Prater was awoken at much the same time when her kitten was disturbed by a noise. But she went back to sleep again.

At 10.45 a.m. next morning, landlord John McCarthy sent Thomas Bowyer to collect Mary Jane's rent – she still owed thirty shillings. Receiving no reply when he knocked at the door, Bowyer lifted back a piece of coat that had been placed there to keep the draught out, and peered through the broken window-pane. What he saw inside caused him to summon his employer to come straight away.

McCarthy arrived, running.

Through the broken pane they witnessed a truly vile spectacle.

Two lumps of flesh could be seen on the bedside table. On the bed lay a mutilated body.

'Go at once to the police station and fetch some one here,' McCarthy told Bowyer.

Bowyer raced off and returned with Inspector Walter Beck who squinted through the window, just as they had done.

Beck immediately despatched a telegram to Superintendent Thomas Arnold. Another telegram was sent to Sir Charles Warren to bring bloodhounds in order to trace the murderer.

At 11.15 a.m. police surgeon Dr Thomas Bond arrived, followed fifteen minutes later by Inspector Frederick Abberline, who gave orders that nobody should be allowed to enter or leave Miller's Court.

Two hours afterwards, Superintendent Arnold instructed that the door of No.13 be broken open with a pickaxe.

The crime scene was so hideous that full details were not reported in newspapers at the time. Mary Jane's throat had been deeply cut, she had been completely disemboweled and her entrails placed on the table. All the skin had been carved from her thighs and abdomen. Her nose had been cut off, her face gashed, and her neck severed down to the bone. Between her feet lay her liver. Her breasts had been cut off: one of them had been placed with her uterus and kidneys under her head, and the other breast was next to her right foot. Her heart had been extracted. In spite of a thorough search of the room it could not be found. It seemed that the killer had taken it away with him.

Pieces of clothing, including a woman's bonnet, were found burned in the grate. Perhaps this had been done to give her killer some light by which to see what he was doing, there being only one small candle in the

Police photograph of Mary Jane Kelly's body on the bed at 13 Miller's Court. (Wikimedia Commons)

room – the candle Mary Jane had bought that morning – which stood on top of a broken wine glass.

The police converged on Miller's Court and cordoned off the area, but that did not stop crowds of onlookers arriving.

That afternoon newsboys cried out: 'Another 'orrible murder!'

At 4 p.m. a horse and cart clattered into Dorset Street, passed under the arch, and pulled up at the entrance to Miller's Court. Two men took down an open shell coffin, which the police instructed them to carry inside.

A long time passed before they emerged, and loaded the coffin back on to the cart to take it away to Shoreditch Mortuary.

As darkness descended, the windows of No. 13 were boarded up, and the door padlocked.

* * *

When Joe Barnett arrived at the mortuary he found her body so mutilated that he could only recognise Mary Jane by her hair and blue eyes.

At the inquest, which opened at Shoreditch Town Hall on 12 November, it was revealed that his former partner was 'the wife of a man from whom she is separated'. Her friend Julia from Miller's Court corroborated this, stating that she had once confided to her that her husband was still alive.

The press reported that Mary Jane was the least wretched and most attractive victim of Jack the Ripper, 'an aristocrat among street women', with well-to-do friends', and who 'led the life of a lady'.[26]

On Monday 19 November, the day of Mary Jane Kelly's funeral, men, women and children from the East End came out of their homes and lined the streets in a great wave of sympathy towards the young, twenty-five-year-old woman who had been murdered so savagely. Dozens of police constables had been drafted in to keep law and order. And yet, ten days earlier most of the crowd had never even heard of the woman they had come to pay their respects to.

Despite extensive newspaper coverage, no relations had come forward to arrange and pay for the funeral. Joe Barnett could not afford the cost, so Mr H. Wilson, sexton at St Leonard's Church, Shoreditch, had agreed to meet it himself.

As the church bell began to toll midday, the crowd that had gathered outside the mortuary gates began to swell. Scores of women were present, several from the pubs Mary Jane had frequented, drawn there by sadness and grief.

As her polished oak and elm coffin appeared, borne on the shoulders of four men, some mourners surged forward in an effort to touch it as it passed. Men removed their hats, while women with tears streaming down their faces shouted: 'God forgive her.'[27]

East London was brought to a standstill as Mary Jane's coffin was carried slowly through the streets towards St Patrick's Catholic Cemetery, Leytonstone, in a glass-sided hearse drawn by two black-plumed horses.

The coffin, engraved 'Marie Jeanette Kelly', was covered with wreaths of artificial flowers sent by her friends from the pubs where she was a regular.

Two mourning carriages followed the hearse on its six-mile journey. Joe Barnett and two other women sat in the first; while the other conveyed five women, all 'unfortunates' who had prepared for the funeral by fortifying themselves with drink.

As they reached the suburbs, the crowds began to thin and the horses were able to break into a trot.

At two o'clock the procession entered St Patrick's churchyard, where a large gathering had assembled. The carriages passed through the gates, which were locked behind them, denying the crowd entry while the burial service was taking place. At the chapel door they were met by Father Columban, a cross bearer, and two other officials.

Mary Jane Kelly's coffin was carried to the northeastern corner of the cemetery, to a pauper's grave. As Father Columban read the service, Joe and the women who had accompanied him, knelt by the graveside and wept.[28]

Conclusion

Mary Ann Nichols, Annie Chapman, Elizabeth Stride, Catherine Eddowes and Mary Jane Kelly were not merely the Ripper's victims, but complex human beings with their own tragic stories that need to be told.

Each of these women ended up living a miserable existence, hand-to-mouth in the slums of London's East End, where, it was said, the sun seldom rose. For them, there was no knowing what the next day would bring: perhaps a few pennies from a little cleaning, selling a few flowers or pieces of crochet. But perhaps it would bring nothing at all.

Their only possessions being the clothes they stood up in, maybe a broken mirror, a comb, and a piece of soap, they had no choice other than rent a room in the cheapest and most squalid of dwellings in a damp tenement with filthy backyard, or share a dormitory with scores of others in a common lodging-house.

Having made few close friends during their transitory lives, these women's final moments on earth were desperately sad affairs, and their funerals, paid for by others, were sparsely attended.

What happened to them during the course of their lives had been defined in large part by the fickleness of fate – unemployment, abandonment, homelessness, or the death of a parent, husband or child.

These women had fallen through the all-too-many gaps in the welfare provision of the day. There were no benefits for them to claim in order to supplement their low wages, and no family allowances. Trade unions for the masses, which might have campaigned for better working conditions, shorter hours and higher pay, were still in their infancy. In theory, the workhouse provided a safety net in an extremely bleak set up, but in practice that institution was associated with fear, shame and humiliation.

Initiatives by philanthropists such as George Peabody, who provided homes for respectable working people, offered a few crumbs of comfort for those who had not already been drawn under and sucked into a whirlpool of misfortune from which there was no escape.

Today we would expect the government to intervene by providing a robust system of welfare measures, including unemployment benefit, affordable housing, public health, old age pension and a funeral allowance.

However, in the *laissez-faire* Britain of the late nineteenth century, individuals tended to be viewed as responsible for their own lives and welfare. The role of the government was primarily to maintain law and order, and to protect the country from invasion. Too great an involvement in social issues would have been deeply unpopular with the middle classes because it implied tax increases.

Old ideas died hard. Poverty was seen as unfortunate but inevitable. Some middle-class people continued to believe – or chose to do so – that it was a crime, caused by individual moral failure, particularly idleness and drunkenness, and that anyone could escape it through self-help, which involved education and, above all, hard work.

It took the surveys of Charles Booth in London (1886–93), and Seebohm Rowntree in York (1899–1901) to shock people into realising the full scale of poverty. There were vast numbers of poor – comprising up to thirty per cent of the population – who were susceptible to chronic illnesses and early death. Their research demonstrated that the causes of poverty were often beyond an individual's control, and that people could not pull themselves out of their wretched situation without help. Meagre wages and uncertain hours of work made it especially difficult for women to lead a regular life, and drove some into prostitution. Without emancipation, and a vote – which women were to be denied for at least another thirty years – they could do little to set about improving their position.

Already impoverished and vulnerable, the victims of the Whitechapel Murderer easily succumbed to weaknesses that are common to all of us. They thought of quick fixes to try to alleviate their condition, placed unwarranted trust in strangers, stole if the opportunity arose, and resorted to drink as a source of comfort.

Today, we can often correct our mistakes, and perhaps even learn something on the way. But for these women their mistakes brought them to the very brink, and had devastating consequences.

* * *

After the death of Mary Jane Kelly, the murders and mutilations came to an end, giving rise to the belief that the murderer may have escaped abroad, committed suicide, or had been put in prison or into an asylum. Within a few months, the hysteria evoked by what has become known as the 'Autumn of Terror' began to dissipate. The all-too-regular yells of 'Murder'; 'Another of 'em'; and 'Mutilation', came to an end. Although the police pursued their enquiries into the winter, they scaled down the search for Jack the Ripper.

By the following spring, amateur patrols were disbanded. But whenever a woman was murdered in Whitechapel over the next few years, no matter how she had been killed, there would be fresh cries that Jack the Ripper was back.

The horrifying living conditions exposed by this grisly episode led to some of the worst slums being pulled down and courtyards being better lit, but nothing changed as far as the lives of working-class women were concerned. The underlying reasons why some became desperate enough to place themselves in such vulnerable and dangerous positions on the streets were never addressed. Governments remained blind to the living and working conditions of poor women, and did not listen to what they had to say.

In 1981 Peter Sutcliffe, the 'Yorkshire Ripper', was sentenced to life imprisonment for the murder of at least thirteen women throughout northern England between 1975 and 1980. Just like the London police forces in 1888, the Yorkshire police were also criticised for their crass and ham-fisted handling of the case. Sutcliffe's victims, like those of Jack the Ripper, were often treated by the media and the public as incidental, and were reduced to a tableau of nameless faces, with no individuality. TV and radio bulletins simply referred to them as 'prostitutes', rather than, say, teachers or dentists; while police working on the case referred to the victims as 'good-time girls' and 'women of loose morals'. In other words, their whole lives were being defined by something that they had turned to in desperation to make ends meet. In reality, they were daughters, mothers and girlfriends, who had been reduced to drinking heavily, and some of them had from time to time sold sex as a way of surviving. Until an 'innocent' sixteen year-old victim was discovered, there was indifference and little public sympathy when the bodies of these 'non-innocent', marginalised women were found. As in 1888, the blame was placed on them for a set of events they were believed to have brought on themselves.

Conclusion

To this day, the risks associated with prostitution have barely changed. According to the *British Medical Journal*, women trapped into selling sex in the UK have mortality rates six times higher than the general population, and are eighteen times more likely to be murdered. Investigators are just beginning to expose their wretched lives. Like Jack the Ripper's victims, these women deserve their hidden stories to be told.

Notes

Introduction
1. Melville Macnaghten. *Days of My Years* (London: Edward Arnold, 1914) pp.55–56
2. Pauline Tarnovsky, 'Anthropological Study of Prostitutes and Female Thieves' (1889), quoted in N. Rafter, ed. *The Origins of Criminology* p.179.

1. Mary Ann Nichols
1. Charles Andrew Cross, eyewitness, at the inquest, *The Times*, 4 Sept. 1888. p.8, cols e and f.
2. *The Illustrated Police News,* 8 Sept. 1888. p.1, centre left.
3. 1851 Census.
4. 1861 Census.
5. https://www.bl.uk/victorian-britain/articles/health-and-hygiene-in-the-19th-century
6. The iconic spire of St Bride's Church in Fleet Street is thought to be the inspiration for the tiered wedding cake.
7. https://www.ncbi.nlm.nih.gov/pmc/articles/PMC3865739/
8. Franklin Parker. *George Peabody. A Biography* (Vanderbilt Univ. Press, 1995) pp.103–109; 124–128.
9. Ibid. p.109.
10. From a small, one-press firm, William Clowes had merged with Caxton Press in 1873, to become one of the world's largest printing companies.
11. *Circle* 11 Apr 1874.
12. Christine Wagg. 'George Peabody and Polly Nichols', *Ripperologist* No.100 ii, Mar. 2009.
13. Years later, future Deputy Labour Leader, George Brown, who was born in Block I, Tenement 22, before moving to another estate,

also berated the fact that washing and toilet facilities had to be shared, but added that, in those days, the Peabody estate was 'a great improvement on the hovels they replaced'. George Brown *In My Way* (Penguin, 1972) p.17.

14. *East London Observer,* 8 Sept. 1888 p.6, col.d
15. Inquest, Day 2, *The Daily Telegraph*, 4 Sept. 1888, p.2, col.g.
16. Lambeth Workhouse Admission and Discharge Registers, London Metropolitan Archives, Microfilm X102/169, X102/170, X113/008, X113/009, X113/010, X113/011; 'A Lambeth Guardian'. The New Pauper Infirmaries and Casual Wards (London: Frederic Norgate,1875).
17. Simon Fowler. *The Workhouse: The People, The Places, The Life Behind Doors* (Pen and Sword, 2014) p.67.
18. Matrimonial Causes Act (1857).
19. Inquest, Day 2 *The Daily Telegraph*, 4 Sept. 1888 p.2, col.g.
20. Much as British doctor and writer William Acton (1857) maintained that some women 'stray from the paths of virtue' by being 'exposed to temptation'.
21. Inquest, Day 1, *The Daily Telegraph,* 3 Sept. 1888 p.3, col.g.
22. *South London Chronicle. and Southwark and Lambeth Ensign,* 5 June 1886 p.6, col.b
23. Charles Dickens. *Sketches by Boz* (1836) Ch.12.
24. http://www.workhouses.org.uk/StGiles/StGiles1881.shtml#Inmates
25. http://www.workhouses.org.uk/Strand/
26. *The Illustrated London News,* 13 Feb. 1886 p.24.
27. http://spartacus-educational.com/TUbloody.htm
28. http://www.workhouses.org.uk/Holborn/
29. Lambeth Workhouse Admission and Discharge Registers, London Metropolitan Archives, Microfilm X102/169, X102/170, X113/008, X113/009, X113/010, X113/011.
30. Cited by Paul Begg. *Jack the Ripper. The Definitive History* (London: Routledge, 2004) p.107
31. 1861 Census documents Francis Cowdry (b.1855 in Bolsover, Sussex) living in Farningham Kent, with his father, Samuel, and mother, Sarah. *Kelly's Directory of Wandsworth, Putney and Tooting,* 1888, 1889, 1890, 1891, 1893 records Samuel Cowdry, who worked as a clerk with the Metropolitan Police, living at 16 Rosehill, and Francis Cowdry living at 18 Rosehill ('Ingleside').

32. 1881 Census.
33. The aim of *Beeton's Book of Household Management* (1861) was to provide men with such well-cooked food at home that it may compete with what they could eat 'at their clubs, well-ordered taverns, and dining-houses'.
34. https://www.pinterest.com/pinniey/jack-the-ripper/
35. *East London Observer,* 8 Sept.1888 p.6, col.a.
36. Inquest, Day 2, *The Daily Telegraph*, 4 Sept. 1888 p.2, col.g.
37. http://www.victorianlondon.org/professions/dressmakers.htm
38. Seth Coven. *Slumming: Sexual and Social Politics in Victorian London* (Princeton NJ: Princeton Univ. Press, 2004)
39. Bracebridge Hemyng. 'Prostitution in London' in Henry Mayhew et al. *The London Underworld in the Victorian Period* (Mineola, NY: Dover Publications, 2005) p.30.
40. http://spartacus-educational.com/Samuel_Barnett.htm
41. *The People of the Abyss* (1903) (London: The Workhouse Press, 2013) p.1.
42. R. Russell. *London Fogs* (1880) (Gloucester: Dodo Press, 2009).
43. *The People of the Abyss* (1903) (London: The Workhouse Press, 2013) p.3, 7, 24.
44. Bronwen Walter. 'Irish/Jewish diasporic intersections in the East End of London: paradoxes and shared locations.' https://core.ac.uk/download/pdf/77282833.pdf (Anglia Ruskin Research Online, 2010)
45. Jack London. *The People of the Abyss* (1903) (London: The Workhouse Press, 2013) p.137.
46. Cited in Eileen Yeo and E.P. Thompson. *The Unknown Mayhew* (New York: Pantheon Books, 1971), p.145.
47. Bracebridge Hemyng. 'Prostitution in London' cit. p.24, 25.
48. Under the terms of the 1885 Criminal Law Amendment Act, a citizen could report to the police any house suspected of operating as a brothel, in return for a reward.
49. *Prostitution, Considered in Its Moral, Social, and Sanitary Aspects* (1857) (1972 edn) p.32n, 39–49.
50. Fiona Rule. *The Worst Street in London* (Shepperton: Ian Allan, 2010).
51. Judith R. Walkowitz. *City of Dreadful Delight. Narratives of Sexual Danger in Late-Victorian London* (London: Virago, 1992) Ch.7.
52. *Tower Hamlets Independent,* 19 Nov.1881, quoted in Jerry White. *London in the 19th Century* (Harmondsworth: Vintage, 2008) p.323

53. Leonard Matters. *The Mystery of Jack the Ripper* (London: Hutchinson,1929).
54. Microfilm of burial register, London Metropolitan Archives Ms.10445/33, register entry No. 210752.
55. *Lloyds Weekly Newspaper,* 9 Sept. 1888 p.3, col.c.
56. 1901 Census. They lived at 41 Bird and Bush Road, Camberwell, and had four children: Arthur, Ethel, Henry and Winifred.

2. Annie Chapman

1. *Illustrated London News*, 27 Sept. 1845, Issue 178, p.208.
2. booth.lse.ac.uk/map
3. *Windsor and Eton Express,* 24 Apr. 1830 p.1, col.a.
4. 1861 Census.
5. Today the church is a Russian Orthodox cathedral.
6. *The Daily News,* 10 Sept. 1888. p.5, col. g.
7. Society for Promoting Legislation for the Control and Cure of Habitual Drunkards.
8. David Cannadine. 'The Victorian binge drinkers. A Point of View', BBC News, 2 Dec. 2005 http://news.bbc.co.uk/1/hi/magazine/4493442.stm
9. *The People of the Abyss* (1902) (London: The Workhouse Press, 2013) p.164.
10. Charles Booth. *Life and Labour of the People in London* (1903), vol. 17, p. 59.
11. The Habitual Drunkards' Act, 1879, offered a retreat to those people whose addiction to intoxicating liquor endangered themselves or others, or who were incapable of managing their affairs.
12. https://en.wikipedia.org/wiki/Sir_Francis_Barry,_1st_Baronet
13. https://historicengland.org.uk/research/inclusive-heritage/disability-history/1832-1914/the-daily-life-of-disabled-people/ https://www.academia.edu/1688653/Degenerates_and_Idiots_Social_Class_and_Epileptology_in_Victorian_Britain
14. This was probably the National Hospital for Diseases of the Nervous System in Queen Square, Bloomsbury.
15. Alan Gillie. 'The origin of the poverty line', *Economic History Review*, XLIX, 4 (1996) pp. 715–730.
16. *The Bitter Cry of Outcast London. An Inquiry into the Condition of the Abject Poor* (1883) p.9 https://archive.org/stream/bittercryofoutca00pres#page/8/mode/2up

17. Inquest, Day 1, *The Daily Telegraph*, 11 Sept. 1888, p.3, cols c and d.
18. *The Daily Telegraph*, 27 Sept. 1888. p.2, col.g
19. Inquest, Day 1, *The Daily Telegraph*, 11 Sept. 1888, p.3, col.d.
20. Ibid.
21. Laurie Graham. *The Night in Question* (London: Quercus, 2015) p.104.
22. Ibid.

3. Elizabeth Stride

1. Anna Lundberg. *Care and Coercion. Medical Knowledge, Social Policy and Patients with Venereal Disease in Sweden, 1785–1903* (Report No. 14, Demographic Data Base, Umeá University, 1999). For syphilis more generally, see Deborah Hayden. *Pox: Genius, Madness and the Mysteries of Syphilis* (New York: Basic Books, 2003).
2. Later renamed Holtermanska Hospital.
3. In the hospital ledger she is entry No.97, and was living in Philgaten in the growing working class suburb of Östra Haga.
4. *Ripperology: The Best of Ripperologist Magazine* (ed. Paul Begg) pp.46–48.
5. According to Michael Kidney, Inquest, Day 3, in *The Daily Telegraph,* 4 Oct. 1888 p.5, col.e.
6. Inquest, Day 4, reported in *The Daily Telegraph,* 6 Oct.1888 p.3, col.a.
7. Clerkenwell Prison, Dec. 1867. During the 'Dynamite Campaign' the Fenians carried out a co-ordinated attack on the London Underground (1883), and planned to blow up Tower Bridge, the House of Commons and the Tower of London (1885).
8. Markman Ellis. *The Coffee House. A Cultural History* (London: Weidenfeld & Nicolson, 2004).
9. *The People of the Abyss* (1902) (London: The Workhouse Press, 2013) p.125.
10. John Lock. *The Princess Alice Disaster* (London: Robert Hale Ltd, 2013).
11. 1881 Census.
12. Inquest, Day 3, *The Daily Telegraph,* 4 Oct. 1888, p.5, col.e.
13. Money book of Swedish Church.
14. Martin Levy. *Doctor Barnardo: Champion of Victorian Children* (Stroud: Amberley Publishing, 2013).
15. Barnardo in a letter to *The Times,* 9 Oct. 1888. p.4, col.f.

16. *The Star,* 1 Oct. 1888 p.2, quoted in Dave Yost. *Elizabeth Stride and Jack the Ripper* (Jefferson, NC: McFarland & Co., 2008) p.57
17. Inquest, Day 3, *The Daily Telegraph,* 4 Oct. 1888, p.5, col.e.

4. Catherine Eddowes

1. Unable to write his name, her father left his mark on Kate's birth certificate.
2. Mike Rapport. *1848: Year of Revolution* (London: Abacus, 2009).
3. 'blue baby syndrome'.
4. M.G. Jones. *The Charity School Movement; a Study of Eighteenth Century Puritanism in Action* (Cambridge: Cambridge Univ. Press, 1938).
5. http://www.workhouses.org.uk/Bermondsey/ In 1881, Sarah Ann is living in the Metropolitan District Asylum For Imbeciles in Caterham, Surrey: 'Sarah Ann EDDOWES Patient Unmarried Female 30 No occupation' (Census Return).
6. http://www.barnardos.org.uk/barnardo_s_children_v2.pdf
7. http://www.workhouses.org.uk/SouthMetSD/
8. Stephen Halliday. *The Great Stink of London. Sir Joseph Bazalgette and the Cleansing of the Victorian Metropolis* (Stroud: History Press, 2013).
9. 1861 Census.
10. http://www.wolverhamptonhistory.org.uk/work/industry/japanning/old_hall
11. Kate gave her address as the workhouse, and registered the baby under the surname Conway.
12. *The Times,* 10 Jan. 1866, p. 12, col. e.
13. "Kidney' Kate Eddowes', *Black Country Bugle,* Jan. 1995, quoted in www.casebook.org/dissertations/
14. The birth was not registered.
15. 1871 Census.
16. http://www.workhouses.org.uk/Southwark/
17. https://www.thejacktheripperwalk.com/victims/
18. A. M. Phypers. *The House Where Jack Swilled? An Investigation of Pubs, Beer & The Ripper* http://www.casebook.org/dissertations/dst-pubsv.html
19. Judith R. Walkowitz. *City of Dreadful Delight. Narratives of Sexual Danger in Late-Victorian London* (London: Virago, 1992) p.194
20. http://wiki.casebook.org/index.php/Flower_and_Dean_Street

21. Elwyn Jones (ed.) *Ripper File* (London: Barker, 1975) p.51
22. http://www.workhouses.org.uk/Whitechapel/
23. Hilary Heffernan. *The Annual Hop. London to Kent. Archive Photographs.* (Stroud: History Press, 1996).
24. Cited in Paul Begg. *Jack the Ripper. The Uncensored Facts* (London: Robson Books, 1988) p.115
25. http://www.workhouses.org.uk/CityOfLondon/parishes.shtml
26. Alex Werner. *Jack the Ripper and the East End* (London: Chatto & Windus, 2012) p.145
27. Hanging around on a street corner would cause police to become suspicious. To escape arrest, prostitutes would parade around the island on which the church (known as the 'Church of Prostitutes') was situated.
28. Inquest, Day 2 *The Daily Telegraph,* 12 Oct. 1888, p.2, col.e.
29. Ibid.
30. The National Archives, HO 144/221 /A49301C: Report by Chief Inspector Swanson regarding Metropolitan Police knowledge of the Mitre Square murder (6 Nov. 1888).
31. Deposition of Dr F.G. Brown, City Police Surgeon, as quoted in Philip Sugden. *The Complete History of Jack the Ripper* (London: Constable & Robinson, 2006) p.244
32. Paul Voodini. *Jack the Ripper, Conan Doyle, & Houdini* (lulu.com, 2015) p.76; 'thousands of people lined the streets,' according to *The Leeds Mercury,* 9 Oct. 1888 p.3, col. d.
33. http://www.mkheritage.co.uk/bfhng/docs/Jul10%20The%20 Victorian%20Funeral.htm
34. Rose Collis. *Death and the City* (Brighton: Hanover Press, 2013) p.20.
35. Microfilm of burial register, London Metropolitan Archives Ms.10445/33, No. 211190.

5. Mary Jane Kelly

1. *The Daily Telegraph*, 13 Nov. 1888 p.5, col.b.
2. Roman Catholic Registers, 1863 and information from Sharon Slater, Limerick Archives. Other sources, if they give a date, cite 31 March, others 25 August https://www.findagrave.com/cgi-bin/fg.cgi?page=gr&GRid=1847. *The Limerick Chronicle,* 10 Nov. 1888, is far from convinced that she was a native of Limerick: 'A rumour prevailed in Limerick today that the murdered woman

was in some way connected with the city, where it is said her parents at one time resided; but this may be found to be one of those vague reports which are so freely circulated on occasions such as this'.

3. *Henry & Coghlan's Directory,* 1867 pp.377–94
4. James S. Donnelly. *The Great Irish Potato Famine* (Stroud: The History Press, 2002); Charles River Editors. *The Irish Potato Famine: The History and Legacy of the Mass Starvation in Ireland During the 19th Century* (CreateSpace Independent Publishing Platform, 2014).
5. David Egan. *Coal Society: History of the South Wales Mining Valleys, 1840–1980* (Welsh history teaching materials,1987).
6. *The Real Mary Kelly* (London: Blink, 2015) pp.29–35.
7. Deposition of Joseph Barnett, Inquest, Day 2, as quoted in *The Daily Telegraph*, 12 Nov. 1888, p.5, cols f and g.
8. A.S. Aldis. *Cardiff Royal Infirmary, 1883–1983* (Cardiff: Univ. of Wales Press, 1984)
9. *Portrait of a Killer* (2002) and *The Secret Life of Walter Sickert* (2017). Cornwell suggests that Sickert had a hole in his penis, and probably had corrective surgical procedures as a child. This traumatic experience transformed him into a mass murderer. Amongst other incriminating evidence, she cites rare watermarks on letters sent to the police by the Ripper, which match those on Sickert's mother's notepaper. Although recognising that there is very little evidence of where Sickert was, or what he was doing during any given day, Cornwell is convinced that he was in Whitechapel in the autumn of 1888, whereas most historians place him in France at the time of the murders.
10. *The Real Mary Kelly* (London: Blink, 2015) pp.37–49.
11. http://www.messynessychic.com/2012/12/11/inside-the-paris-brothels-of-the-belle-epoque/
12. Booth's poverty maps.
13. *The Real Mary Kelly* (London: Blink, 2015) p.56.
14. Ibid. p.59.
15. Ever since *Harris's List of Covent Garden Ladies* (1757–95)
16. *The Real Mary Kelly* (London: Blink, 2015) p.76.
17. Ibid. p.19.
18. Ibid. p.15.
19. Ibid. p.16.
20. Fiona Rule. *The Worst Street in London* (Shepperton: Ian Allan, 2008) pp.12–13.

21. *The Sun,* New York, 10 Nov.1888. p.1, col.a
22. *Eddowes's Journal*, 14 Nov. 1888, p.5, col.b. The *Dublin Evening Mail* described her lodging as 'an outhouse or shed', 9 Nov. p.3 col.d.
23. *The Fisherman's Widow* by Charles James Lewis (1830–92).
24. Tom Cullen. *Autumn of Terror: Jack the Ripper His Crimes and Times* (1945) (Fontana Books, 1966), cited in John Smithkey III http://www.casebook.org/victorian_london/tenbells.html
25. The Right Honourable James Whitehead, the new Lord Mayor, would process through the streets in his state coach, drawn by six horses, and attended by his chaplain, sword-bearer and mace-bearer.
26. Quoted in L.W. Matters. *The Mystery of Jack the Ripper* (London: Hutchinson,1929) p.243
27. James Marsh. *The Funeral of Mary Jane Kelly* http://www.casebook.org/dissertations/rip-funeralmjk.html
28. Ibid.

Bibliography and Further Reading

Ackroyd, Peter. *London, The Biography* (London: Chatto and Windus, 2001).

Acton, William. *Prostitution, considered in its moral, social and sanitary aspects, in London and other large cities* (John Churchill, 1862).

Arnold, Catharine. *City of Sin. London and its Vices* (London: Simon & Schuster, 2010).

Bartley, Paula. *Prostitution: Prevention and Reform in England, 1860–1914* (London, New York: Routledge, 1999).

Beeton, Isabella. *A Book of Household Management* (S.O. Beeton, 1861).

Begg, Paul. *Jack the Ripper. The Uncensored Facts* (London: Robson Books, 1988).

Begg, Paul. *Jack the Ripper. The Definitive History* (London: Routledge, 2004).

Begg, Paul, Martin Fido and Keith Skinner. *The Complete Jack the Ripper A–Z* (London: John Blake, 2010).

Begg, Paul and John Bennett. *Jack the Ripper. The Forgotten Victims* (New Haven: Yale University Press, 2013).

Booth, Charles. *Life and Labour of the People in London: East, Central and South London* (London: Macmillan & Co.,1903).

Chesney, Kellow. *The Victorian Underworld* (Harmondsworth: Penguin, 1989).

Clark, Robert and Philip Hutchinson. *The London of Jack the Ripper. Then and Now* (Stoke-on-Trent: Breedon Books, 2007).

Cornwell, Patricia. *Portrait of a Killer. Jack the Ripper. Case Closed* (London: Little, Brown, 2002).

Cornwell, Patricia. *Ripper. The Secret Life of Walter Sickert* (Seattle: Thomas & Mercer, 2017).

Coven, Seth. *Slumming: Sexual and Social Politics in Victorian London* (Princeton: Princeton Univ. Press, 2006).

Evans, Stewart P. and Keith Skinner. *The Ultimate Jack the Ripper Sourcebook* (London: Robinson, 2000).

Evans, Stewart P. and Keith Skinner. *Jack the Ripper. Letters from Hell* (Stroud: Sutton Publishing, 2001).

Fishman, W.J. *East End 1888.* (Nottingham: Five Leaves Publications, 2nd edn, 2005).

Fuller, Jean Overton. *Sickert and the Ripper Crimes: 1888 Ripper Murders and the Artist Walter Richard Sickert* (Oxford: Mandrake, 2003)

Graham, Laurie. *The Night in Question* (London: Quercus, 2015). Historical novel about the life of Catherine Eddowes.

Horn, Pamela. *The Rise and Fall of the Victorian Servant* (Dublin: Gill and Macmillan, 1975).

Jackson, Lee. *Dirty Old London. The Victorian Fight against Filth* (Yale: Yale University Press, reprinted 2015).

Jakubowski, Maxim and Nathan Braund (eds). *The Mammoth Book of Jack the Ripper* (London: Robinson, 1999).

Jones, Elwyn (ed.) *Ripper File* (London: Barker, 1975)

Jones, Richard. *Jack the Ripper: The Casebook* (London: Andre Deutsch, 2008).

Knight, Stephen. *Jack the Ripper: The Final Solution* (London: Harrap, 1976)

Lavender, Veronica. *Jack the Ripper and the Ghost of Mary Jane Kelly, Born 1863 – Died 1888* (Createspace Independent Pub., 2014).

Law, John. *A City Girl. A Realistic Story* (London: Authors' Co-operative Publishing Co.,1887)

London, Jack. *The People of the Abyss*, 1902 (London: The Workhouse Press, 2013).

Marshall, Dorothy. *The English Domestic Servant in History* (Historical Association, 1949).

Mayhew, Henry. *London Labour and the London Poor* (Harmondsworth: Penguin, 1985).

Mayhew, Henry et al. *The London Underworld in the Victorian Period* (New York: Dover Publications, 2005).

O'Neill, Joseph. *The Secret World of the Victorian Lodging House* (Pen and Sword, 2014)

Perring, William J. *The Seduction of Mary Kelly* (Kindle, 2005).

Perry Curtis, L., Jr *Jack the Ripper and the London Press* (New Haven and London: Yale University Press, 2001).

Preston, W.C. *The Bitter Cry of Outcast London. An Inquiry into the Condition of the Abject Poor* (London: James Clarke & Co.,1883).

Picard, Liza. *Victorian London. The Life of a City 1840–1870* (London: Phoenix, 2005).

Rubenhold, Hallie. *The Five: The Untold Lives of the Women Killed by Jack the Ripper* (New York: Doubleday, 2019)

Rule, Fiona. *The Worst Street in London* (Hersham: Ian Allan, 2008).

Rumbelow, Donald. *The Complete Jack the Ripper* (Harmondsworth: Penguin, 1988).

Sheldon, Neal S. *The Victims of Jack the Ripper* (Edmonton: Inklings Press, 2007).

Stubley, Peter. 1888. *London Murders in the Year of the Ripper* (Stroud: The History Press, 2012)

Sugden, Philip. *The Complete History of Jack the Ripper* (London: Constable and Robinson, 1994).

Trow, M.J. *Jack the Ripper: Quest for a Killer* (Wharncliffe True Crime, 2009).

Walkowitz, Judith R. *City of Dreadful Delight. Narratives of Sexual Danger in Late-Victorian London* (London: Virago, 1992).

Walkowitz, Judith R. *Prostitution and Victorian Society. Women, class, and the state* (Cambridge: Cambridge University Press, 1982).

Warwick, Alexandra and Martin Willis. *Jack the Ripper. Media, culture, history* (Manchester: Manchester University Press, 2007).

Werner, Alex. *Jack the Ripper and the East End* (London: Chatto & Windus, 2012 edn).

Weston-Davies, Wynne. *The Real Mary Kelly* (London: Blink, 2015).

White, Jerry. *London in the 19th Century: 'A Human Awful wonder of God'* (Harmondsworth: Vintage, 2008).

Wilson, Colin and Robin Odell. *Jack the Ripper. Summing up and Verdict* (Harmondsworth: Corgi Books, 1987).

Wise, Sarah. *The Blackest Streets. The Life and Death of a Victorian Slum* (Harmondsworth: Vintage, 2009).

Yost, Dave. *Elizabeth Stride and Jack the Ripper. The Life and Death of the Reputed Third Victim* (Jefferson, NC: McFarland & Co., 2008).

Index